Cover : Garland of flowers and leaves made from card covered in silk thread. Archive piece from the early 19th century. Maison Roze silk velvet.

Back cover : Bell-pull tassel, Hôtel de la Marine. Fabric by Tassinari and Chatel.

TRIMMINGS

DECLERCQ PASSEMENTIERS'S MASTERY OF EXCELLENCE

PHOTOGRAPHS BY
ALEXANDRE RÉTY

TEXT
CATHERINE DEYDIER

PREFACE BY
RAPHAËLLE LE BAUD

ABRAMS / NEW YORK

CONTENTS

Ivory, chrome and silk tieback, on
an ivory silk faille curtain, with
a border featuring embroidery by Lesage,
following a design by Josef Hoffmann.
By François-Joseph Graf.

Declercq Passementiers, radical elegance

―――――

My abiding memory of my visit to Declercq Passementiers' workshop is the sound of the wooden looms, which have been faithfully playing this music, creating fringes, gimps, and braids, for 170 years. Of course I also remember the craftspeople. Olivier, who has been working there for 32 years, wearing his belt adorned with reels of thread. Dominique's feel for color and ability to take any reference and reproduce it exactly, mixing different shades of silk, cotton, and viscose thread. The radio murmuring away in Isabelle and Anne-Sophie's room, where their fingers perform an elaborate dance as they cover the wooden molds in silk. I also think of the upright piano in Elisa Declercq's office. You can hear it being played during breaks, or in the morning, before the song of the looms has begun. If she had not joined the family business with her brother, Jérôme Declercq, she would have been a professional pianist. This sense of what might have been shows just how strong the influence of the family legacy is.

It all began without any fanfare. A man set up his own passementerie business. His daughter carried it on. Her husband took over. Their son grew the business while living through three wars, recognizing the importance of passing on traditional skills so that the craft of passementerie would survive first industrialization, then the move toward more standardized interior design.

Passementerie is a typically French touch of elegance.

The best interior designers know how to use it, whether they are working on cultural heritage sites or in modern interiors. These chameleon-like pieces contrast with, emphasize, or accentuate a curtain, an armchair, or a couch.

Margot Declercq, Jérôme's daughter, joined the family business at the age of twenty. She has worked across all the crafts in the workshop, slowly learning how to embrace this legacy, as the seventh generation working in the family business. "The biggest challenge is to make sure that this craft is kept alive, that it is not forgotten."

That is why the Declercq family wanted to tell the story of their craft in this book. From thread to decoration, from father to daughter. So that each reader may understand this elegance, this commitment to beauty, and become an ambassador for passementerie.

Raphaëlle Le Baud
Entrepreneur in the fine crafts sector
Founder of The Craft Project podcast and Métiers Rares

Left: Cushion with a border of fringe with silk wicks. Fabric by Verel de Belval. Tieback with woollen bobbles and love knots; red silk tieback from the Louis XIV era. Background painted by Stéphane Declercq. *Following double page, left:* Fringe with silk pendants and double gimp with cord, by Tassinari & Chatel; *right:* Tieback with leaf pattern made from covered card. Designed by François-Joseph Graf.

THE THREAD OF HISTORY

Versailles, Fontainebleau, Compiègne, Chantilly, Hôtel de Beauharnais, Hôtel de la Marine... Each and every stunning project completed to the highest professional standards showcases the importance of these unique skills, this craftsmanship passed down from one generation to the next. From thread to decoration, passementerie provides the finishing touch that elevates a room.

CABINET DE LA MÉRIDIENNE, CHÂTEAU OF VERSAILLES.

Decorative bow made of fabric by Tassinari & Chatel, with a *duchesse* border.
Center with *a chardon bouclé* design of curled threads surrounded by loops.

"The word 'passementerie' comes from [the French] 'passement,' meaning a strip of fabric made with gold, silk, wool, or cotton thread and used to embellish clothing, furniture, or wall hangings," explains Évelyne Baron, curator of regional cultural heritage for the Museums of the Seine-et-Marne Department, in her book *Et le ruban prit du galon*[1].

THE UNIVERSE OF PASSEMENTERIE

The craft—called "passamaneria" in Italy and "passamen" in Provence—evokes a universe of elegance and refinement. An art whose "origin is to be found in textile fringes," as Maggy Baum and Chantal Boyeldieu write in *Le Dictionnaire des textiles*. "The art of passementerie goes hand in hand with textile manufacturing. Tying the warp threads at the end of the weaving process sometimes makes the pieces more durable but above all its function is decorative. It embellishes, enriches, adds movement and life to the fabric or clothing,"[2] as would be shown to great effect in the Middle Ages.

The art of passementerie consists of weaving or interlacing threads in narrow strips, but, "more broadly, the term passementerie refers to the industry dedicated to creating all the adornments and embellishments that are added to pieces of fabric," explains Évelyne Baron. "It is not simply a question of braids and ribbons created on looms, but also of tassels, fringes, and a variety of three-dimensional elements requiring different production techniques, many of which are made by hand."[3]

1. Évelyne Baron, *Et le ruban prit du galon*, Saint-Cyr-sur-Morin, Musée des pays de Seine-et-Marne, 1998.
2. Maggy Baum, Chantal Boyeldieu, *Le Dictionnaire des textiles*, Lille, Éditions du Paillié, 2006.
3. Évelyne Baron, *Et le ruban prit du galon*, op. cit.

Display case in Declercq Passementiers' archives.

Opposite: Handwoven
snail-shell gimp made from
guipure and Milanese fabric.

Bottom: Wide braid made
from wool and silk.

Below: Braids from Declercq
Passementiers' collection.

The elegant adornments of passementerie have been used around the world since the days of Ancient Egypt, but it was in the West that the craft took on its most varied forms. In Europe, where passementerie sits on the border between the worlds of fashion and interior decoration, the craft began to grow in the twelfth century and reached its height in the nineteenth, during the Second French Empire. But before these craftspeople were called passementiers, as Évelyne Baron writes, there were trade associations for crépiniers (from crépine, a kind of fringe made of woven gold threads and used as an embellishment), for craftspeople working with gold thread, for dorelotiers (named after a type of passementerie that has since fallen into disuse), and for sayetteurs (Flemish weavers who worked with sayette, a mixture of wool and silk). Then, in 1404, the ribbon-workers appeared, who wove fringes and ribbons. These ribbon-workers were separate from those who worked with needles (who at the time were passementiers), thimbles, crochet hooks, or spindles. "In 1637, they took on the name of passementiers, button-workers and embellishers. In 1653, they became passementiers, fabric workers and embellishers," before the French Revolution spelled the end for trade associations. "In 1784, the passementiers finally started to use looms."

As time passed, the craft evolved, industrialized, and became more sophisticated. It started to draw on weaving, embroidery, knotting, and sewing, as well as the work of goldsmiths. The techniques used to create the pieces were divided into different categories: weaving, which was carried out on vertical looms, horizontal looms, or looms equipped with Jacquard machines; twisting; and hand-finishing for the adornments that were solely created with a needle (tiebacks, tassels, rosettes...) by établisseuses (so-called because they worked at benches, called établis in French). It was the era of embellishers, weavers and twisters...

Works of passementerie abounded in the second half of the nineteenth century, riding the unprecedented wave of enthusiasm and artistic flourishing during the French Second Empire. Pieces made of silk, cotton, or wool thread were highly sought after to adorn private homes, with tiebacks, tassels, braids, and hangings for chandeliers, as well as frogging, ribbons, and braids for ceremonial dress all reaching the height of their popularity. The bourgeoisie seized on these outward signs of wealth as a way to open up new possibilities for themselves and attain a certain status. From then on, passementerie grew and diversified, successfully following the latest fashion trends.

Despite this success, the understated approach that came to dominate decorative arts in the early twentieth century meant that passementerie fell out of fashion, to the point where it was almost forgotten. The craft was in gradual decline until, in recent decades, the restoration of royal apartments and national châteaux—Versailles, Fontainebleau, Compiègne, and Chantilly to name but a few—ushered it back into center stage. And the great interior designers brought it right up to date.

THE CHÂTEAU OF VERSAILLES

◆

The Palace of Versailles is the most beautiful setting to showcase the creations of French artisans and craftspeople. In the private apartments, the textiles and passementerie that decorate the furniture in the King and Queen's bedroom are the first elements that you notice. In the Cabinet de la Méridienne, one of the most private places in the château, where Marie-Antoinette liked to rest and entertain friends, the passementerie is just as remarkable. Declercq now has its own workshop dedicated to these restoration projects, which require specific expertise.

MERCURY SALON.

Above, top: Curtains embellished with a handwoven double gimp made of gold lamé and fine fringe. *Bottom:* Detail of a cushion from a folding stool. *Right:* Folding stool with a velvet cushion, gold lace fringe, a braid with a fleur de lys design, and rosettes with gold tassels.

THE QUEEN'S GOLD CHAMBER.

Above, left: Detail of the bed in an alcove, with a gold braid, gold gimp, decorative bow, and gold and green tassels with jasmines. Fabric by Prelle. Upholstery by Michel Chauveau and Sébastien Ragueneau. *Top right:* Ceiling decoration with leaves made from covered card and gold fleur de lys, braid with torsades and jasmines. *Bottom right and opposite:* Double gimp with gold rope and a gold braid on an armchair and chair. Fabric by Prelle. Upholstery by Michel Chauveau and Sébastien Ragueneau.

THE QUEEN'S BEDCHAMBER.
Details of the bed, fringe, and tassels with torsades and jasmines featuring cannetille migrets, a decorative bow,
a garland of leaves and peas made from card covered in silk. Brocade by Prelle.

THE QUEEN'S BEDCHAMBER.
Detail of a bolster, rosette made from loops of fabric, and checkered button, with two tassels with jasmines and torsades.

Emmanuel Lelièvre

Director of Tassinari & Chatel

As well as a collection of more than 6,000 items—from fabrics to accessories—Lelièvre Paris boasts one of the oldest silk weaving companies in Lyon, Tassinari & Chatel, which traces its history back to 1680 and was acquired by Lelièvre in 1998. The company knows how to balance traditional craftsmanship—such as weaving exceptional brocades by hand—with embracing innovation. Clearly a fitting partner for Declercq Passementiers.

"I have known Jérôme Declercq since 2010. At that time we were both members of the CSTA, the French association of soft furnishings. We soon started working on projects together, particularly via Tassinari & Chatel. At that time, we were often commissioned by conservators to work on the same restoration projects… although we didn't always know it," Emmanuel Lelièvre recalls with a smile. "Outside of the work that we do together on pieces commissioned by museums, we also represent the Declercq Passementiers in certain markets. Versailles, the Mobilier National, the Opéra Garnier… the projects that we have been asked to work on in France are very important to us, but so are our projects elsewhere in Europe and in the United States, whether it is a historic monument or a private château.

We also have our own cultural heritage department which oversees the restoration of pieces and looks after our archives. We have an ongoing dialogue with Declercq. We are interested in each other's work and want to see each other flourish. We have to work together very closely. If we are restoring a piece together, it is important that we can coordinate between ourselves on site to find the best suppliers, to work with the same colorways, the same gold, etc. All of these details are essential. The third man, who adds the finishing touches to our work, is often Rémy Brazet [Maison Brazet]. We have a very good working relationship, and the most striking proof of this may be our restoration of the Cabinet de la Méridienne, Marie-Antoinette's chamber in the Château of Versailles. We also worked together at Chantilly and the Hôtel Beauharnais, where we provided exceptional silks woven in our studios. We are very proud of these."

CABINET DE LA MÉRIDIENNE, CHÂTEAU OF VERSAILLES.
Silk fringe in shades of mauve, green, yellow, and cream, with jasmines and torsades, fan-edged border and *corde à puits*, decorative bows and two tassels. Fabric by Tassinari & Chatel. Upholstery by Sébastien Ragueneau.

A
FAMILY
SAGA

From the first humble factory that was opened in 1852 on rue Quincampoix, through rue Saint-Sauveur to the current showroom a stone's throw away on rue Étienne Marcel, the story of this family business goes back seven generations. A hundred and seventy years of bespoke craftsmanship, of preserving a cultural heritage, refining the secrets of production, passing a passion on from father to daughter, from mother to son... The stories of men and women, professionals, who kept this grand tradition alive, preserving their unique expertise, conscious of their responsibility as the guardians of precious knowledge, inimitable craftsmanship that provides the finishing touch for exquisitely refined interiors. These craftspeople forged paths across the whole world, while never abandoning the corner of Paris that has always been the home of passementiers.

ARTISANS OF A CRAFT BETWEEN PAST AND FUTURE

Make no mistake, the guardians of this extraordinary expertise were shaped by the times they lived through, which forced them to adapt to the emergence of a new era. Ensuring that they were able to pass on their legacy, while still embracing innovative techniques and drawing on other disciplines, that has always been the challenge facing each new generation. Now more than ever. Each generation inherits the responsibility to breathe new life into these skills, to create something new, but above all to reinvent these treasures in a way that appeals to the prevailing tastes of the day; to share their experience of hours spent at the loom, the pleasure of touching an exceptional piece, of exploring the perfect union of art and craftsmanship. To help people understand and experience the force that guides their hand toward creativity, innovation, modernity, and instinctive understanding.

Jacqueline Perret-Declercq (right) and her cousin Christiane standing in front of La Passementerie Nouvelle's shop on rue des Petits Champs in Paris, in 1926.

The first in this line of passementiers was born in 1832. Joseph Bertaud founded the House, a small family-run workshop that made pieces to order for its customers. His only daughter, Marie-Louise, who was married to Ernest Perret, worked alongside her father, then naturally took over from him. As well as creating pieces of passementerie in the workshop, she enjoyed going to meet suppliers and clients. It also made sense for Ernest, who had sold lace and ribbons before meeting her, to move into passementerie. Marie-Louise was less than 40 years old when she became ill and had to pass the reins on to her son Gaston, who was married to Marguerite, a trainee seamstress working for Jeanne Lanvin, and the daughter of upholsterers Édouard and Désirée-Augustine Lointier, who were based in Cité Vaneau. Luckily, Marie-Louise's diagnosis proved incorrect and she lived far longer than her doctor had predicted. This meant she was never far away, always able to offer her expertise and support to the young couple who had taken over running the business. Young Marguerite had chosen to join Gaston and help run the workshop during this period of instability, shaped by the impact of the Great War, the economic crisis of the 1920s, the emergence of Art Nouveau, and a new professional world that was moving away from passementerie.

However, Gaston Perret was not the kind of man who would give up at the first sign of trouble. In 1927, he developed and patented the little flounce, a braid used as a fringe. This saved the business. La Passementerie Nouvelle was born and the family saga was set in motion. While their days were marked by the rhythms of the workshop, the family also knew how to enjoy life's little pleasures. Gaston never missed a chance to play his accordion or go boating on the Marne. The couple often took the train to the Bastille to stay at their house on the island of Fanac, near Joinville-le-Pont. Their only daughter, Jacqueline, grew up in a happy, creative, and productive environment. And when the time came, in 1948, the young woman took over the reins of the business, with her husband Marcel Declercq. As well as giving the company his name, this friendly businessman, who was well liked by everyone, had an in-depth understanding of the other side of interior decoration, as his own father, an upholsterer, had shown him the ropes.

Jérôme Declercq, the current president of the company, who belongs to the sixth generation, adds, "It was my father, Claude, the son of Jacqueline and Marcel, who built the House's enduring reputation and success."

Family portraits showing (*top to bottom, left to right*): Joseph Bertaud, Marie-Louise Bertaud, Ernest Perret, and Gaston Perret.

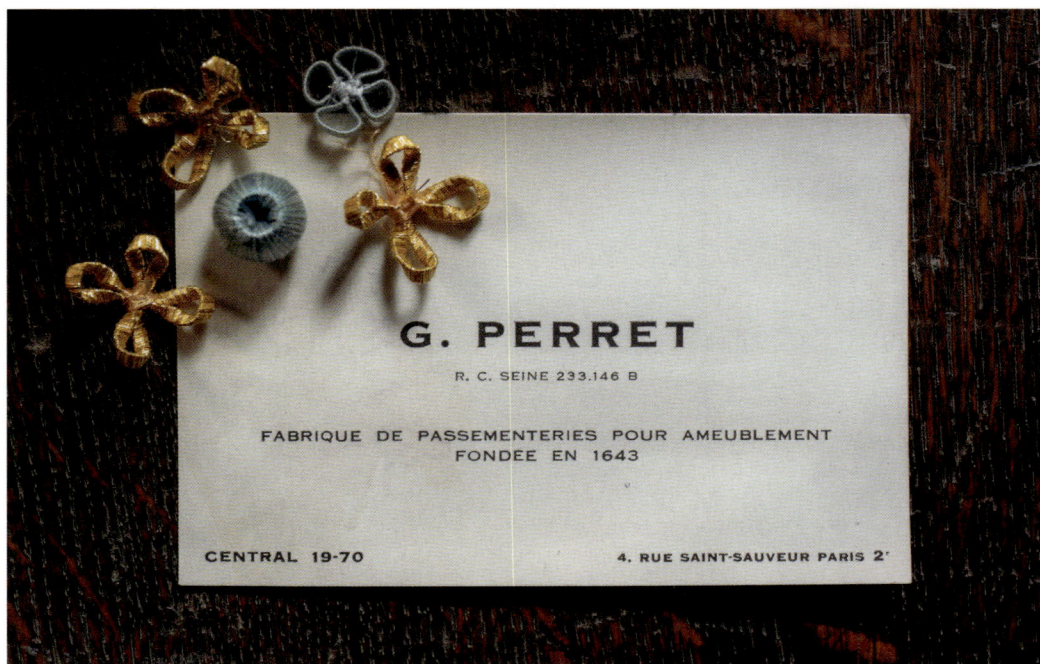

Left: The little flounce created by Gaston Perret in 1927. *Above:* A question of history. Officially, Joseph Bertaud bought the factory and set up his passementerie business in 1852. However, Jérôme Declercq has discovered a business card from 1930 belonging to his great-grandfather Gaston, which says, "Passementerie business founded in 1643." This may explain why there are tiebacks that date from the reign of Louis XIV and other pieces from the 17th century in Declercq's archives.

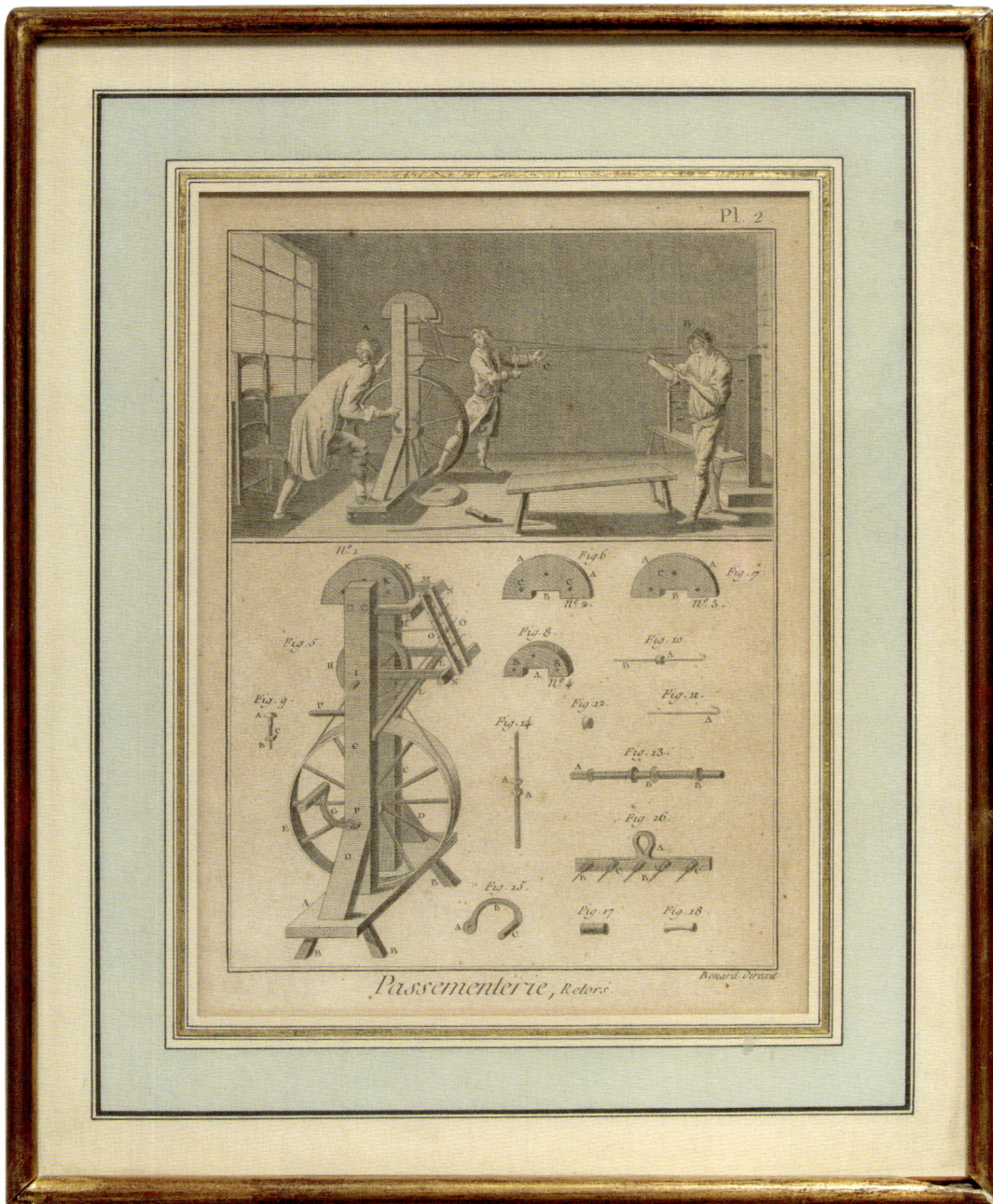

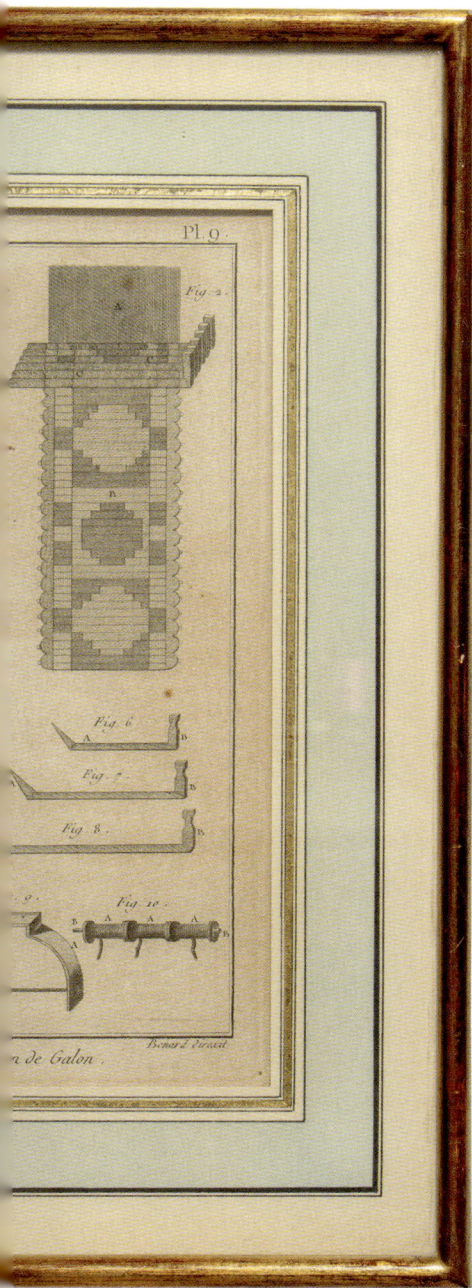

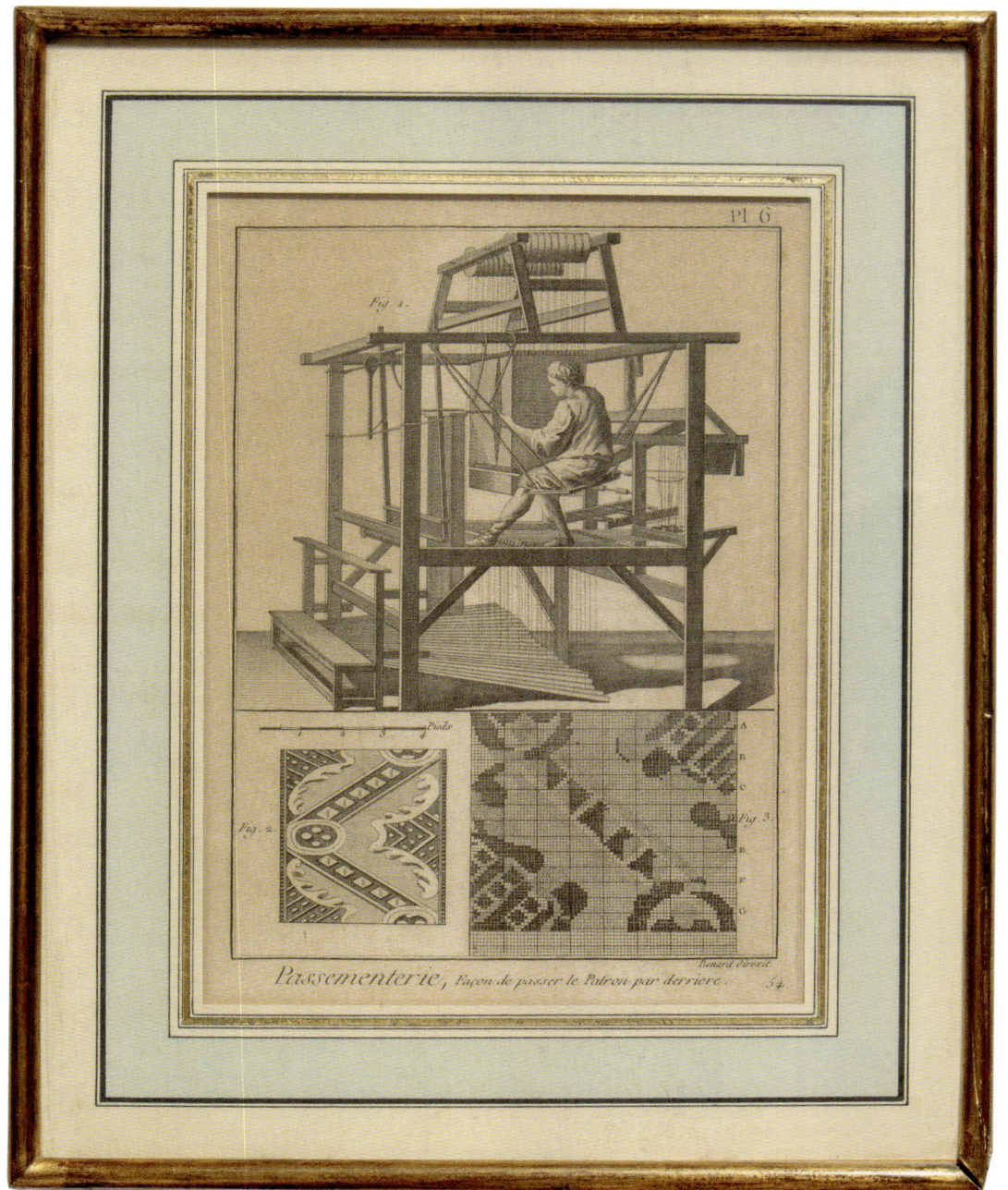

Diagrams about passementerie taken from Diderot and Alembert's Encyclopedia.

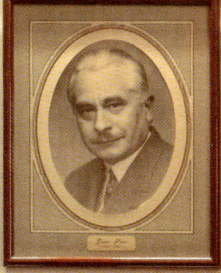

"Joseph was an errand boy and peddler before joining the passementerie business, which he later managed. Marie-Louise, his daughter, started out as a salesgirl. Then she met Ernest, a lace and ribbon salesman. Gaston's cheerful demeanor saw him through two wars and the Great Depression of 1929. It was he who created the little flounce that saved the company after the war."

Declercq Passementiers' shop at 15 rue Étienne-Marcel in Paris.

Above: Portraits of Marcel Declercq and Jacqueline Perret-Declercq. *Right:* Declercq Passementiers' shop at 15 rue Étienne-Marcel in Paris.

Left: Gimps from Declercq Passementiers' collections. *Above:* Sample book from the archives.

"He designed a lot, he was an unrivaled colorist. His Macapass collection, for example, was very innovative and still has a very contemporary feel. It combined linen, wool, and string."

CLAUDE DECLERCQ, REVOLUTIONIZING THE HOUSE

Claude Declercq was a true force of nature, with a passion for passementerie from an early age. He trained as a weaver alongside his grandfather, who had a greater influence on him than his father. The workshop held no secrets for him. He did his apprenticeship there, learning about each stage of the production process, down to the smallest detail. The older workers recall that he worked incredibly hard and sometimes came back to the workshop to weave a fringe after his ping pong competitions. Family legend also has it that, during his military service, Claude used his leave to go "looking for customers."

He was the natural heir to this line of entrepreneurs, more than capable of taking over from his father Marcel, who in no way resented his son's role. Quite the opposite. Even at a young age, Claude was not afraid to forge his own path, led by his instincts and dreams. Jacqueline faithfully supported her brave, visionary son, even in his craziest plans. "My grandmother was in awe of her son. They had a very close relationship," Jérôme recalls. "Jacqueline had also started out with her parents, and she was a very good saleswoman in their shop on rue des Petits Champs. She was better than anyone at writing the famous production notes and provided the link between the different crafts. She was the main woman of the House, and many of the customers said they were charmed by her, because she was very charming." With this unconditional support—his mother even worked through the night to help him—Claude built a large and growing business. They only had eight employees when he took over.

Claude, a globe-trotting entrepreneur, also proved to be charming and artistic. Above all, he enjoyed letting his imagination run wild and traveling the world, from the countries of the East to the furthest reaches of South America. His prodigious energy allowed him to concentrate on multiple projects at once. "He designed a lot, he was an unrivaled colorist. His Macapass collection, for example, was very innovative and still has a very contemporary feel. It combined linen, wool, and string." The influence of this "larger-than-life" giant was felt everywhere.

Claude Declercq at his loom.

PILGRIM OF PASSEMENTERIE

From the early 1960s onwards, Claude Declercq expanded the workshop, earning the passementerie business the status that it still enjoys today. The times were favorable. Within the space of a few years, he was offering a range of collections, and he also followed his instincts to invest in an iconic part of French cultural heritage. "In 1972, he acquired the very old House of Louvet & Mauny, which dates back to the nineteenth century, a jewel of our profession. Thanks to this acquisition, we expanded our archives, adding very rare, exciting documents from different eras. In 1977, he bought another prestigious House, André Boudin, to which we owe the most beautiful passementeries from the early twentieth century," explains Jérôme Declercq.

As well as traveling through time, Claude also traveled across the world to spread the word about his craft, his gifts, and his creations, making a name for the business on the international stage. His ambition proved fruitful. In the 1990s, Michael Jackson asked this family of musicians to create the epaulettes for one of his stage costumes. And the American artist was well known for his meticulous approach to his costumes!

Claude's fellow travelers were Pierre and Patrick Frey, Manuel Canovas, and Jack Lenor Larsen… Talented partners in crime who were at the forefront of the interior design world, exhibiting great freedom and flair. They created trends in textiles, set the tone, and breathed new life into domestic spaces in the 1970s, embracing the era's lively, light-hearted, pop-culture feel. Their brave stylistic experiments gleefully broke with the conventionalism that reigned in the profession at the time. Their research into color, designs, and shapes brought modernity and a breath of fresh air that led to other writings, new contrasts, and a certain flamboyance. Just like, among others, Claude.

Claude, a composer in his spare time, performed for his friends on his famous green piano—which his daughter Elisa kept for many years in her office at the factory—as well as playing around and noting down his songs on it between trips. He was never without his accordion, which he played in hotel rooms while traveling for work. It was a passion that never left him, a passion inherited from Gaston, his grandfather.

In the shop's gallery, he put on exhibitions of work by artists from Eastern Europe, whose paintings he was particularly fond of, as well as presenting his own tapestries and avant-garde three-dimensional woven pieces. On rue Étienne Marcel, he also gave private concerts, during which the guests did not hesitate to sing along. It was like a family orchestra, "true Parisian folk music." "We even recorded a double album and a single. Cabu designed the cover, a suspicious-looking rabbit sneaking into an enormous tank, because a rabbit will always try its luck," Jérôme recalls with a smile. He loves talking about his father, "about his energy, his creations, his sense of color, his instinct for business." For example, Claude created collections made up of pieces that were kept in stock, thereby opening up the world of passementerie to a wider range of customers.

Left: Belt-style tieback made of braid, designed by Serge Olivares. Braid woven by Jacquard, diamond design made of chenille, flower with chardon around the center, made of silk velvet. *Top:* Portrait of Claude Declercq.

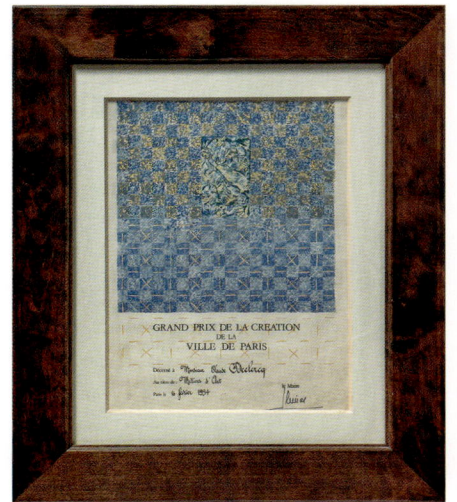

Patrick Frey

Publisher, fabric and wallpaper designer

"In 1969, when I returned from studying my craft in the United States, I joined my family business. When my father introduced me to Claude Declercq, we immediately got on well. Although at first he worked with my father, we then worked on a number of projects together, and over the years we shared a wonderful friendship. Claude explained that, when he was starting out, he simply asked my father if he could 'hitch his wagon to ours to present his passementeries.' It was unheard of at the time to present a passementerie collection with matching fabrics. We put him in touch with Manuel Canovas, who was a close friend. I must admit, our small world was just ticking over, and Claude shook it up. He used our creations as a starting point, offering ranges that followed the colorways of Frey and Canovas, so that we could present pieces that went together. The sales representatives' work had already been done for them. He also created his own designs, calling himself 'a parasite who thrives thanks to the work of the Houses.' Soon all three brands had the same sales network, and this joint product line did very well in the market for many years. This approach shook up our way of working a little but it was very enticing because it was a breath of fresh air. We were bringing passementerie up to date everywhere, and Claude had truly made his name. He was like a king. He revolutionized this craft and was undoubtedly a leading light in the field.

I must say that Claude—a man who was artistic director, creator, and business owner all at once—was a fantastic character. He liked to party, he had a feel of Cyrano de Bergerac, while still being very modest. Working with him was such a pleasure.

He had a very well developed, very clear artistic vision and a huge amount of talent. He was original, curious about everything, joyful, larger than life, like a character from a Rabelais novel. He had a love of sailing, which was clearly a source of inspiration. He was at the châteaux, the museums; he traveled a lot, especially to the United States, where he had started to establish a foothold for the business before conquering the Middle East and Russia. He was one of the first to visit the Arabian Gulf and forge partnerships there, also one of the first to set up factories in Asia and Africa.

I had a certain respect for him. We always remained loyal to each other, working together. Our customers appreciated this close relationship. Declercq embraced the influence of interior designers and talents such as Manuel Canovas, who was an unrivaled master of color. Everyone appreciated his taste and sensibility. He had a close working relationship with [American textile artist] Sheila Hicks, who, I think, showed him how to imagine pieces that he perhaps would not have dared to create otherwise.

Declercq had incredible archives and collections and the craftspeople in his workshops had the magic touch. We didn't see each other very often socially, as we did not have the same lifestyle, but he lived his life to the full and passionately pursued his craft.

I knew him with Marcel and Jacqueline, on rue Saint-Sauveur, then when he was running the business on his own. None of his competitors produced such beautiful work. His unique personality made him, undoubtedly, a great man in his field."

Château of Bagatelle, Polish bed. Fabric by Braquenié and matching passementerie.

Claude Declercq, "a master craftsman of passementerie, singer, and sailor on the high seas," a man with a passion for culture, history, and literature, passed away in 2016 at the age of 86, at peace, but still brimming with ideas and dreams despite his illness.

PASSING ON THE TORCH

His son Jérôme had learned his trade in the building on rue Saint-Sauveur, which had three stories: the shop, the workshop, and the floor where his grandparents lived. As a child, he was constantly roaming between the floors and was often on the looms, but his father watched over him and kept a careful eye on his bespoke training. Claude saw his role as that of a patriarch. He was proud of his son, although he didn't go easy on him.

At the age of 10, the young boy announced, "I'm going to be the President and Director General of La Passementerie Nouvelle!" It was a promise he kept. Today, Jérôme Declercq runs the family business, which he officially started working for at the age of 18, after finishing school. He had a deep-rooted desire to follow in the footsteps of his father, his grandmother, and the five generations that had gone before him. He started out with a two-year apprenticeship at the workshop in Montreuil-aux-Lions, where he learned handweaving, twisting, and mechanical weaving. Then, he continued his apprenticeship at the workshop on rue Saint-Sauveur, where he was paid "on a piecework basis," like the other production workers. He looks back on these years very fondly. "I was happy to see Claude and Lucien every morning. There was a carefree atmosphere there. My rabbit, Cerise, roamed freely around the Parisian workshop. Then, when it came time for people to retire, that was very difficult for me. I felt a bit like an orphan, I was losing part of my work family." Next, Jérôme spent a further two years learning about the intricacies of business on rue Étienne Marcel, before being sent abroad, first to Germany, then to work for Dupin in Geneva and Guy Evans in London. He traveled with the sales representatives and spent three months at Brunschwig & Fils in New York. All wonderful adventures that took him around the world, with stopovers in Thailand, Japan, Korea, Australia, and Russia. But New York, Switzerland, and the Arabian Peninsula remained unequivocally his father's domain. That didn't matter, though; Jérôme enjoyed working with new people. "I don't like spending time alone, I like being around other people. Walking was my way of understanding. It gave me time to make decisions, to form opinions. I made a place for myself, claimed my ground, and set up the brand Declercq Passementiers." He did so with the support of his sister Elisa, who still runs the workshop today. Their father, a man of few words, said only, "We will see the results and the failures." Message received.

Left: Jacqueline Perret-Declercq with her son Claude and her grandson Jérôme. *Center:* Claude Declercq with his children Jérôme and Elisa. *Right:* Jérôme, Margot, and Elisa Declercq.

Jérôme designed his very first piece, a decorative tassel for the renowned interiors company Mercier, in the early 1980s. His grandmother gave it the green light. When the "Othello" collection was launched, it was a first for him: finally creating an entire product line. Little by little, Claude backed off and began entrusting him with projects. Next, the young man presented "Rêve de Soie," using color pencil to determine the color scheme during his holidays. Next, a set of tiebacks called "Tsarina." The patriarch balked when his son said he wanted to create his own designs. And although Claude gave his approval to produce a collection based on the "Manhattan" tassel—conceived as a Christmas present and designed by Jérôme for their customers—he did not want to sell it, arguing that these famous customers preferred his own creations. The vanity of an artist, perhaps, who was used to calling the shots?

However, the Manhattan tassel is still the piece of which Jérôme is most proud. "My pure creation, Manhattan truly expresses what I love. It's an interpretation of a skyscraper, a mixture of metallic materials and silk in a contemporary shape. It's like a piece of music that you're happy to have composed entirely on your own. I am proud to have created a piece of passementerie that has become somewhat iconic." He always acknowledges the vital role that the Parisian interior designer François-Joseph Graf played from the early days of his career, pushing him to venture outside his comfort zone and experiment with innovative techniques. "I thought I knew the world of passementerie, but Mr Graf showed me that I still had a lot to learn. I will always be grateful to him for that." François-Joseph Graf helped him to finish the "Metropolis" collection, down to the smallest details. This marked the start of a long collaboration between them, which gave Declercq Passementiers the opportunity to celebrate the talents of its craftspeople and add many iconic designs to its catalogue. Other collections included "Oklahoma," "Les Ors," "Lola," and "Théodora"… And when his turn came, Jérôme took over full responsibility for creating new pieces.

The Manhattan tassel, created by Jérôme Declercq, made from steel and silk. *Following double page, left:* Coral tieback, created with Thomas Boog; *right:* Tieback with scales. Fabric by Le Crin. Upholstery by Laurent Jannin and Carla Rodriguez Moreno.

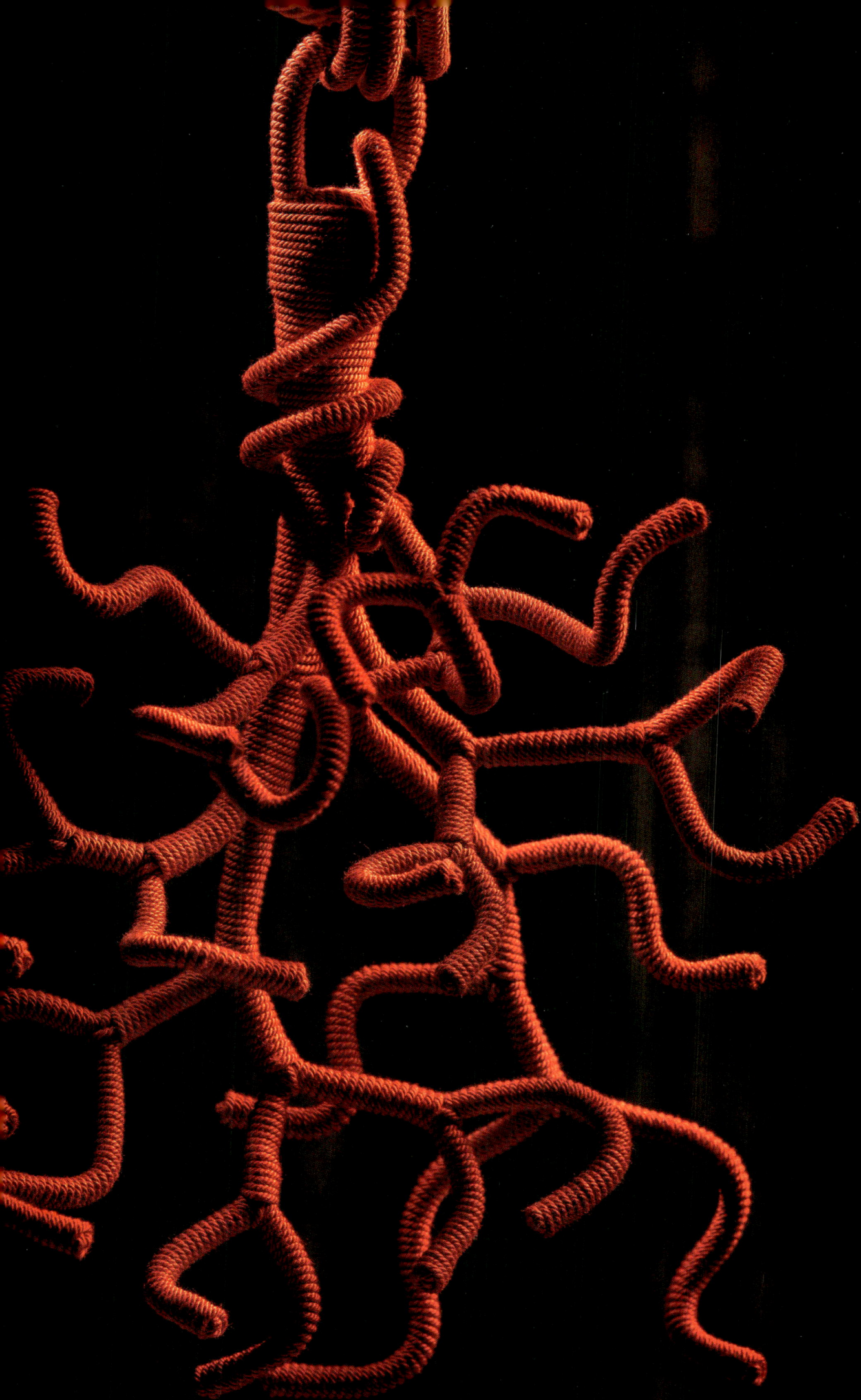

"The elegance of a tieback with torsades, the subtle graphic feel of a rosette... passementerie, the height of sophistication, accentuates the fabric like a precious diamond that sets off a 'little black dress.' You have to get under its skin to fully appreciate its delicate beauty."

———

Alix de Dives

In 1996, the shop's showroom was redecorated. Jérôme transformed the space to give it an atmosphere that was more reminiscent of a "family home." "We completely rethought the shop, giving it a bold new look designed to showcase our collections to their best advantage. I had display cases put in for the museum, so that we could have documents from the past at our fingertips. Having access to these intrigued and reassured our customers. We were also able to personalize the entrance with wall decorations designed and created by my brother Stéphane." The family is always involved, even behind the scenes. Finally, Jérôme turned to the stylist Alix de Dives for his advertising campaigns and to create stands when they showed their work at the Biennale of Decorative Arts at the Grand Palais. The sets, which were sometimes irreverent ("The nuns' refectory"), funny, and often scathing ("The three blows" and "The geese of the Capitol"), went down in history. The pair were daring, shaking up the sometimes fusty image of passementerie and calling for a more hard-hitting conversation. "Alix de Dives helped me a great deal with these projects. She knew how to tell stories with taste, finesse, and a sense of humor."

White armchair. Fabric by Braquenié. Upholstery by La Manufacture. Styling by Alix de Dives.

THE HÔTEL DE BEAUHARNAIS

◆

This private mansion, purchased in 1803
by Eugène de Beauharnais, was classed
as a historic monument in 1951 and is now the
residence of the German ambassador to France.
The renovation work was overseen by
the Center for National Monuments.
For the Salon of the Four Seasons,
Declercq Passementiers created, among other
pieces, fringes with torsades made of gold
and a variety of tiebacks—*roulé, grappé,*
and with torsades—for the majestic curtains,
as well as gold braids and tasseled rosettes
for the couches and armchairs.

Hôtel de Beauharnais.

Salon of the Four Seasons.

SALON OF THE FOUR SEASONS (IN THE STYLE OF THE FIRST EMPIRE).

Fabric by Prelle and Veraseta. Upholstery by Xavier Bonnet. *Left:* Tieback with two tassels with gold torsades.
Right: Cushions with gold silk braid embroidered with daisies. Detail of fringe with gold torsades.

Terracotta Salon (in the style of the First Empire).
The curtains have silk lattice-knot fringes with wicks. Fabrics by Prelle and Veraseta. Upholstery by Phelippeau.

Alexandre Phelippeau

Upholsterer

Following in the footsteps of his grandfather Roger and his father Jean-Paul, Alexandre Phelippeau comes from a long line of weavers, couturiers, and upholsterers, craftspeople who have passed their expertise down from generation to generation, but who also embrace the world of contemporary creativity. And for over thirty years now, Phelippeau Tapissiers have been working with Declercq Passementiers.

"We have always worked together a lot, mainly on unusual projects. We are not in the business of mass production. Like us, they have an extraordinary history, which sets them apart from other suppliers. What is it that makes them different? Their high-end product ranges and their mastery of specific skills. If you want to create beautiful fringes, you need to know the best length to make them, to suit the design, and if we are looking for high-quality materials, whether that is silk or gold, we immediately think of them, without hesitation. It's a matter of trust.

We have recently worked together on the Opéra Garnier, the Hôtel de la Marine, and Versailles. Declercq's wonderful archives—especially from the Louis XVI era and the Second Empire—offer a wealth of inspiration and different interpretations that we can use to create designs that are out of the ordinary.

I admire the unique character of Declercq's products, and the philosophy that Jérôme and Margot are developing together. They always seek to meet the customer's brief exactly. When a client brings us specific documents, we share them with Declercq as soon as possible. This is essential to ensure that we are working together smoothly and making the most of their passementerie skills from the start. Because in the end, whatever happens, it is always a challenge."

Cardinal red velvet curtain with a wide double-gimp border with knots, loops, flowers, and buttons. Corner detail with decorative loops. Fabric blind embellished with jasmines made from molds with *grappé* mesh designs, embroidered by Lesage. Fabric by Tassinari & Chatel. Upholstery by Phelippeau. Designed by François-Joseph Graf.

François-Joseph Graf

Architect, designer and interior designer

The son of an antiques dealer, François-Joseph Graf trained as an architect, gaining his degree from the École du Louvre, and has built a reputation for himself that reaches far beyond the borders of his home country of France. He has worked on a number of restoration projects for the French Historic Monuments Commission, including Versailles and the Trianon, as well as rooms in the Museum of Decorative Arts. His in-depth knowledge is rivaled only by his determination to achieve perfection, down to the smallest detail, and he strives to ensure that passementerie in all its varied forms appeals to contemporary tastes. "There is so much to be explored, but we must not forget everything that has gone before," he says, adding that he looks to the nineteenth century for inspiration.

A sketch, measurements and a three-dimensional creation… François-Joseph Graf, an interior designer, embraces the technical side of his work with great precision. And without compromise. "One day," Jérôme Declercq recalls, "my father told me that he wanted me to meet François-Joseph Graf, saying that there was a great deal he could teach me. In all honesty, I was skeptical because passementerie was my area of expertise. But he was right. Monsieur Graf taught me a great deal and always pushes us to test our limits." Since that first meeting, the two have had many exchanges, and there are even rumors that they might soon release a joint collection.

"Creating something is always a pleasure, no matter what it is. Designing a façade, a door, a fabric, a bag, that is all architecture," says François-Joseph Graf, whose uncompromising artistic vision is legendary. He met Claude Declercq in 1992. "I told him, 'When I become your customer, I will be your biggest customer,' and that is exactly what happened when we started to work for Pierre Bergé. I commissioned him to recreate an extraordinary piece of passementerie that was in their collections." This collaboration was a turning point in Declercq Passementiers' evolution, marking the start of an important partnership for Jérôme, which would lead to creations of extraordinary quality.

"I did not go easy on Jérôme," the interior designer admits, although he was well aware of the challenges of passementerie. "I met him when he was 30 years old and I have definitely always been his most demanding, difficult customer. The commissions were sometimes completely crazy, but the pieces that Declercq created in response were stunning. I remember there were strips of fringe made of wood, for example. Even the padding they make is beautiful, there is something absolutely unique about it." Declercq's other great strength is that "they have priceless archives, which are incredibly well catalogued and indexed." François-Joseph Graf knows how to make the most of this expertise to create interiors that draw the eye to these elegant details, which provide the finishing touches to a room.

Tieback embellished with jasmines made of loops of covered card and satin-covered baubles in different shades, with a trim of fleur de lys and leaves made from covered card around the top. Border woven by Le Manach. Designed by François-Joseph Graf.

Left: Tieback with two tassels, braided rope, molds with criss-cross patterns, flowers with *chardon* bouclé design of curled threads in the center surrounded by loops, bullion fringe, jasmines with loops, double *migrets*, and moulinets, and torsades made of natural silk in two colors. *Above, left to right, top to bottom:* Silk cascade fringe in Art Deco style; Empire-style tieback with pendants and satin-covered baubles, *limacé* with multi-colored checkered pattern; tieback and fringe with jasmines made from baubles, radis, pendants, and satin tassels with *grappé* mesh; armchair fringe made of point de neige lace, with berries and loops in cross stitch. Designed by François-Joseph Graf.

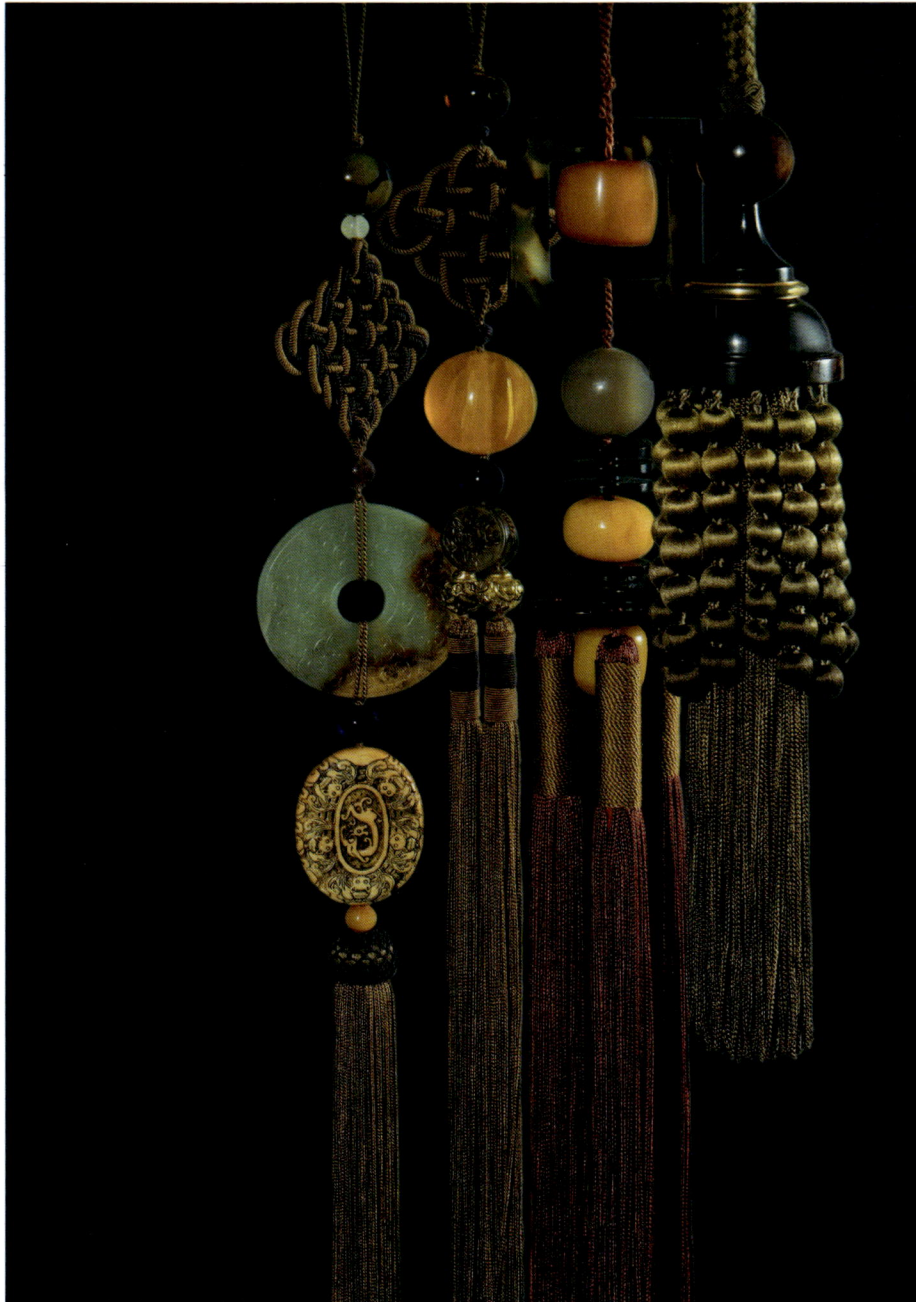

Left: Tassels for tiebacks with amber, jade, tiger's eye, and ebony beads, satin-covered baubles in different shades, and Korean knots. *Right:* Tieback made of woven guipure rope, with gilded metal belt buckles, Chinese stone carvings, Korean knots, amethysts, and coral baubles, on a curtain made of dark blue silk gros de Tours fabric, embroidered by Lesage. Designed by François-Joseph Graf.

Franck Sorbier

Master of Art, couturier, craftsman

"You could say that I seek to reimagine crafts; in my collections, passementerie can become an integral part of the piece of clothing I am designing. The first piece I created with Jérôme Declercq was the wedding dress for the Fall/Winter 2014 collection. The bodice is made of tiebacks, braids, pompoms, everything in a magnificent pastel gray. Unfortunately, such excellent craftsmanship is now a rare sight. And although these embellishments on the dresses seem to give them a museum-like feel, an element of cultural heritage, for me they are clearly part of an approach that looks to the future.

As a Master of Art honored by the French Ministry of Culture, I am very aware of Declercq's cultural heritage, with its incredible archives. I sometimes feel that we belong to a species that is slowly disappearing, the last of the Mohicans. That means we must be good stewards of our craft and push our work as far as possible, saying to ourselves, I must get there, even if the price our work is sold for is not directly proportional to the work involved. We are selling dreams. In couture, at least, you have to preserve an element of mystery, this language that is so specific to textiles…

We also find it in passementerie. In fact, what we have in common is our sense of resistance, our desire to preserve the soul, the spirit of our craft, to embrace an approach that passes on our legacy, to look to those who will come after us. Skill, time, demanding the best… these are important elements that bring richness to our work, both in passementerie and in couture. It was therefore inevitable that our paths would cross. There was a simple, face-to-face meeting between Isabelle (my wife), Bruno Le Page (my right-hand man) and Jérôme, who showed a real curiosity about our work. He listens more than he speaks, but he knows how to ask the right question at the right time, in order to understand if he can supply what we need. I appreciate this honest, authentic exchange.

As for the Declercq showroom, it is a real Ali Baba's cave, a warm place full of knowledge and swatches that go back generations. One day, I found a name among the wreath of flowers. It intrigued me. The design dated back to his father's time. The flowers were perfect for a piece, a Japanese dress with a blue jacket, that I had designed for my collection. Jérôme generously offered us these pieces from his archives so that they could have a new life, an unexpected rebirth."

Fringe with beaded threads used as an embellishment on a dress, designed by Franck Sorbier. 2019 collection.

THE CHÂTEAU OF CHANTILLY

—◆—

A jewel in the crown of French cultural heritage, the Château of Chantilly passed through the hands of a number of princely dynasties. It was Henri of Orléans (1822–1897), Duke of Aumale, who left the strongest mark on the château, as throughout his life he was dedicated to preserving and celebrating its treasures. The Grand Apartments boast extravagant, iconic interiors from the eighteenth century. The formal apartments have perfectly preserved the spirit of decorative arts from the July Monarchy. The passementerie has pride of place, adding a touch of elegance and opulence.

Private apartments, Salon de Condé.

PRIVATE APARTMENTS, SALON DE CONDÉ, IMITATING THE STYLE OF LOUIS XIV,
POPULAR DURING THE JULY MONARCHY.

Above: Tieback with two tassels with *grappé* mesh designs and criss-crosses, embellished with flowers and buttons, with beaded fringe. *Right:* Lambrequin embellished with gold and silk tassels.

ROYAL APARTMENTS, MUSIC ROOM.
Tiebacks with two tassels with *grappé* mesh designs and criss-crosses, embellished with flowers and buttons, with a fringe of twisted threads and torsades. Handwoven double gimp and silk tie.

PURPLE SALON, THE DUKE OF AUMALE'S PRIVATE APARTMENTS.

The Duchess of Aumale's salon was originally decorated in green, but the Duke of Aumale ordered it to be redecorated in purple brocade with silver thread after his wife's death in 1869, because purple is associated with mourning. Small handwoven fan-edged double gimp used as an embellishment on an armchair. On the wall, bell-pull tassel with a silk lattice-knot fringe, with criss-crosses and bands of *chardon bouclé* with curled threads. Silk braid with laurel leaves woven by Jacquard. Fabric by Tassinari and Chatel. Upholstery by Michel Chauveau.

Jérôme Declercq:

Passing on a legacy

Although he no longer spends as much time among the looms in the workshop, Jérôme is still inspired by the music of these timeless machines, the movement of the shuttles, the clattering of the Jacquard machines' suspended cards, the reeds striking the braids and fringes… He admits that he misses going to the workshop. He still enjoys working as part of a team and is fascinated by the production process, the smells, the soft crunching sound of the silk, the balance between fabrics and colors. He is driven by the mysterious force that makes it possible to create pieces, these tiebacks for example, that will stand the test of time. It is impossible not to be reminded of his early days learning alongside those who went before him.

Just as his father did, Jérôme is introducing new innovations, combining new fabrics rather than just natural silk, and allowing memories of his travels to seep in. Surprising touches that celebrate the work of his artisans, weavers, and twisters… He and his sister Elisa are making their own mark on the family legacy, embracing the creative innovations of the twenty-first century. Through their work, Declercq Passementiers is gaining even greater recognition than before. They have been entrusted with a number of restoration projects, both public and private, and special commissions for the Château of Versailles and the grand foyer of the Opéra Garnier in Paris, as well as working on memorable pieces for royal and imperial palaces such as Chantilly and Compiègne.

Today, as the House of Declercq marks its 170th anniversary, Jérôme Declercq recognizes the importance of celebrating the significant moments in the company's past, recording its history so that it can live on: "I am the guardian of this legacy. I can open a window onto our family's adventure. I am the only one who can pass it on today. My father passed this legacy on to me, and it comes with a responsibility. When I first arrived, my grandmother was working alongside her son. Two generations were writing their own surprising chapters in this story, building on the foundation laid down by those who'd gone before them. It is down to me to pass on this legacy, through words and images, and above all through the work we create. I must tell this story. I am only passing through, providing a link between yesterday, today, and tomorrow. It is my responsibility to breathe new life into the House of Declercq's distinctive approach and to drive us forward into the future."

Teaching and sharing techniques and knowledge are top priorities for Jérôme, driven by a passion for the skills he has mastered that inspire the distinctive spirit of creativity at Declercq Passementiers. He is looking to the future, to "passing on the House of Declercq without abandoning it entirely, but also not trying to control everything." Ultimately, his aim is to hand the baton over to the next, seventh, generation, represented today by his daughter Margot. Because, for Jérôme, Declercq Passementiers is still, above all, a story about family.

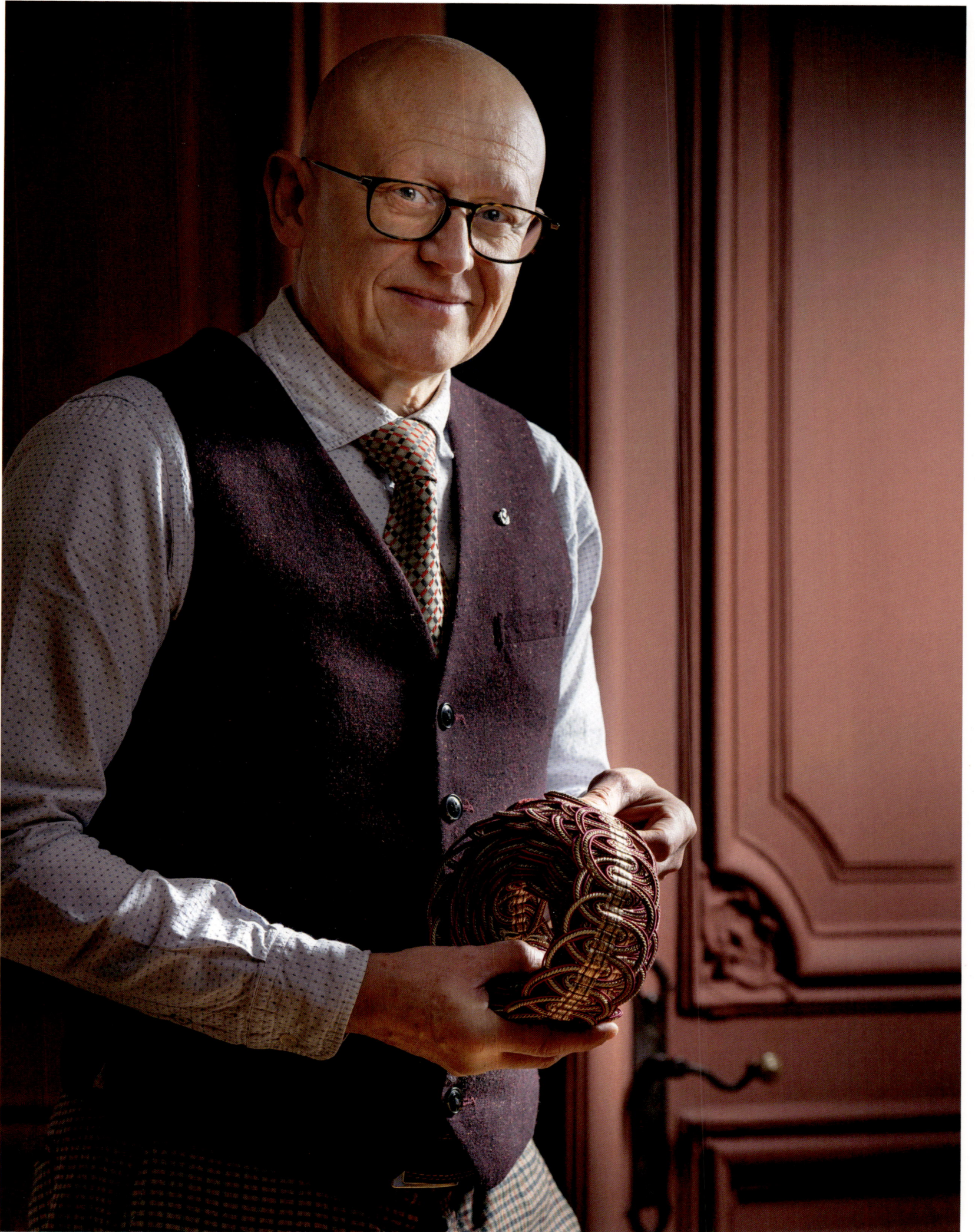

PICKING UP
THE
THREADS

1852

1867

1866

1856

1857

1865

1867

1854

A spirit of productivity reigns
in the workshop in Montreuil-
aux-Lions, the heart of the business,
which Elisa Declercq watches
over day to day. It is in this
modern building, which dates
to the 1970s, surrounded by
fruit trees and rose bushes planted
by the patriarch, that the
twenty-four craftspeople create the
small elements that will make up
the tiebacks, fringes, tassels, braids,
and other gimps. Mastering
these ancient crafts means sharing
expertise and experience,
working side by side to tackle
any problems that may arise.

Molds made of beech wood, used to make tiebacks.

Montreuil-aux-Lions, workshop

When Claude Declercq began presenting four
or five collections each year, that meant pieces
had to be produced on a large scale, hundreds
of tiebacks, rosettes, and fringes... The space on
rue Saint-Sauveur was too small, so he began to
look for a place to set up a workshop nearby.
He was interested in Montreuil-aux-Lions, an area
he already knew well. He employed craftspeople
to work from home there, creating tiebacks
and fringes. And every week, he visited to take
delivery of the pieces he had ordered. At that
time, passementerie was still the main industry
in this small town in the Aisne department, a few
miles from La Ferté-sous-Jouarre, although the
workshops were closing down one by one.
Older people recalled singing while they worked
on Jacquard looms, to keep up a steady rhythm
to their movements, as Évelyne Baron writes in
her book. In the 1970s, Claude Declercq moved all
of his workshops to Montreuil-aux-Lions, and
they have remained there ever since. However,
in the 1980s and 1990s, he also set up a workshop
in Korba, Tunisia, with the help of Leïla Boufaïed.
The workshop is still there and employs twenty-five
people making stock pieces. The workshop
set up in Hanoi, Vietnam, worked with silk for
twenty years, but it was not so fortunate
and had to close down because it was too far away.
The workshop in Egypt suffered the same fate.

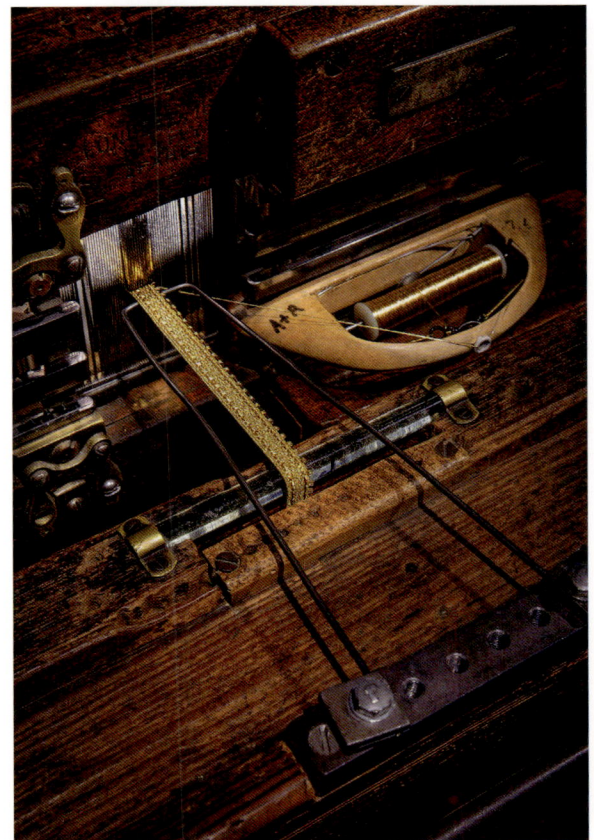

Left: Jacquard machine. *Above:* Braids being woven on Jacquard machines.

The ballad
of Elisa Declercq

Or the dance of the looms

In the Declercq family, every generation is musical. "This culture is passed down from father to son or daughter," confirms Elisa, who now runs the business with her brother Jérôme. No one raises an eyebrow at the drumkit and range of instruments in the basement of the Parisian showroom, but for a long time their father's iconic green piano was abandoned in a corner of the workshop. It was eventually rescued by Elisa, who was the only one in the family to study classical music. A sign of a strong character, who was not afraid to take the road less traveled. When she set up her office in the Montreuil-aux-Lions workshop, Elisa moved the famous piano there. As the days went by, everyone grew used to hearing the boss practice her scales at lunchtime. Nowadays, Elisa practices at home on her Pleyel, and Claude's piano is now in the Ardèche in Camille's house, one of Jérôme's sons.

In the workshop, Elisa is inspired by the rhythm of the looms. She doesn't need to be able to see the machines. She hears them, listening to the work being carried out. She has an ear for it. "Each stage has its own distinctive noises, sounds, rhythms. Some of the machines make a banging noise and have to be handled very carefully, while others make very soft sounds, but with a bit of practice you can recognize them all. Warping, for example. The sound made by all the bobbins unspooling is unique. And the sound of the winding, when you pick the right colors and the cones of thread are placed on the beam. As they unwind, they give off a sound of singing wood," says the multi-tasking Elisa. She explains that the cardboard bobbins used during this stage create a more amusing sound, "as if you are blowing into a bottle." And what about the ballad of twisting? The electric spinning wheel provides an accompaniment, floating above the sound of the twister. She also finds the chorus of brocade-makers, who work with three or four shuttles, deeply moving. Their rhythm is slower because of the old machines. "I love to watch them move. It's almost hypnotic and creates a certain sense of calm," says Elisa. "When we come into the factory, we need to hear this cacophony of small noises, as proof that everything is going well, that the looms are working. It is a sign of life. And although concentration is very important, that doesn't mean silence is the order of the day."

Elisa often stands at the heart of the workshop to help. She listens, to her left, to her right, to the melody of the twenty-two craftspeople at work. From the person soldering to the hand-weaver working on a vertical loom, without forgetting the creaking of the wooden stairs that respond to every movement, the voices, the conversations. "In fact, the ear provides an essential link. Perhaps listening is one of the invisible skills of the passementier," she concludes.

THE IMPERIAL CHÂTEAU OF COMPIÈGNE

◆

The Château of Compiègne, a royal
and imperial residence, was built by
Louis XV and Louis XVI, then refurbished
by Napoleon I and Napoleon III. Its interiors
and furniture include a wealth of rare, exceptional
First Empire items, which pose a challenge today
for the conservators tasked with preserving
these historic apartments, as they seek to recreate
the Empress's Bedroom while remaining
faithful to what is known about it. Sometimes
all they need is a footrest that has been kept
in storage to use as a basis to recreate the original
damask, gimp, braids, and tiebacks.

Empress's Bedchamber (First Empire).

Left: Detail of an 18th-century armchair and a footstool covered with green damask that has been recreated exactly by
Le Manach, embellished with gimps and fine bullion fringe with gold torsades. *Right:* Empress Eugénie's bed in the Élysée Palace.
The green damask curtains and the original passementerie have been recreated exactly.

Details of passementerie created for Empress Eugénie's bed in the Élysée Palace, displayed in the Museum of the Second Empire at the Château of Compiègne. Tieback with tie, leaves made from covered card, and gold torsades. Bullion fringe with torsades, handwoven silk gimp with gold frogging and decorative knots. Fabric by Le Manach. Upholstery by Michel Chauveau.

Rémy Brazet

Upholstery restorer

For more than fifty years, the House of Brazet has been renowned for its work restoring furniture in the collections of the most prestigious museums. "My father had a wonderful touch," explains Rémy Brazet, who took over the business in 1983. He considered becoming an antiques dealer after studying at the École du Louvre but, like his grandmother and his father before him, he became an upholsterer. This was partly thanks to Colombe Samoyault-Verlet, an art historian and head curator at the museum of the Château de Fontainebleau, who "opened his eyes." He made the right choice, as he says, "I could never have imagined that I would enjoy it so much."

Although now more than ever he recognizes the importance of craftsmanship and passing on the skills of upholstery, Rémy Brazet is by no means a stranger to the latest advances. This is clear from his collaboration with the J. Paul Getty Museum in Los Angeles, which led him to design a new removable support frame system for preserving ancient wood during restoration, a system that is still used across the world. However, as an upholsterer, he always comes back to the traditional tools: his needles, leather needles, pins, upholstery hammer, ripping chisel, nail punch, regulator needle, and webbing stretcher.

"In the Declercq collections, we work a lot with the Pleasures of Velvet and the Winter Palace ranges, their handmade silk passementeries. But we don't hesitate to ask them to make pieces to order according to our needs. We have worked together in this way on Marie-Antoinette's bedroom, a historic project in every way, for which we asked them to make pieces of passementerie that drew on the archives and contemporary records.

We recently worked with Declercq on the stool that Edgar Jayet designed. I find it interesting to work with young creators. We listen to them to make sure we can meet their expectations and answer their technical questions, but they are not afraid to push us out of our traditional way of doing things so that we create a finished product that corresponds to what they want to express. Our story with Declercq Passementiers goes back a long way, to the major works at Fontainebleau. Jérôme Declercq and I both embrace an approach that respects expertise and the beauty of the craft. At Declercq, their work is enriched by the memories and stories that we share. They understand the importance of the work done by cabinetmakers and upholsterers. This typically French expertise is part of our cultural heritage. We have a duty and a responsibility to pass it on to the next generation. With this in mind, I am working with Julien Huet, an upholsterer who has been part of our team for fifteen years. I like the idea that, in our craft, we can trace an object's path. That is very important to me. You need to have the patience to wait for these treasures to make their way into public collections, and then they take time to restore a piece according to the techniques used when it was first created."

MUSIC ROOM (IN THE STYLE OF THE SECOND EMPIRE).
Detail of a large padded couch covered in silk created by Tassinari & Chatel. Rosette with leaves made from covered card, two tassels with flowers and jasmines with *migrets*, cannetille, and buttons, gimp with diagonal weave. Upholstery by Rémy Brazet.

Margot Declercq: The next generation

Or rising to the challenge

This lively young woman, in her thirties, has already been working for the family business for more than ten years. However, she studied ceramics and fine arts in Paris and originally planned to pursue a career as an artist. More than once, she questioned whether she wanted to work in passementerie, weighing up her desire to do so with her concerns about throwing herself into the family business. Life is full of surprises, and eventually it didn't take much soul-searching for her to decide to join the older members of her family. She was patient, taking the time to learn about every area, undergoing training like all new employees. Especially in production, under the watchful eye of her aunt. "Elisa made me want to do it. I was lucky enough to be mentored at the workshop and I learned a lot." Watching her move from one loom to the next is enough to prove that beyond any doubt. Like her aunt and her father, Margot Declercq loves working with all the employees in the workshop, who have helped her to discover her strength, her manual skills. She never forgets that "every piece we create is thanks to them. They are constantly testing their own limits." And she recognizes that these precious skills must be preserved, that this inheritance must be passed on, so she is nervous every time someone retires.

After spending five years learning all the different skills in the workshop, the time came for Margot to start shadowing her father. She spent another five years doing so, practicing her scales before taking over the reins, to get an overview of the business… and think about how she would soon be the one tasked with passing on its legacy. Perhaps more than anyone else, she had to be assertive and claim her place in this lineage, among the forebears that she holds in such high esteem. She has had to take on the weight of responsibility from the past, and at the same time embrace her own passion and her desire to take risks. She and Jérôme have found their rhythm, keeping an eye on things together.

For three years now, Margot has been building up her own roster of clients. "Either Jérôme delegates projects to me, or I approach them myself." She has learned how to deal with customers and all sorts of unforeseen issues, which has made her "realize that [her] father has a lot of faith in her," and that there is so much more to this work than she knew. "We are a family business, and today I know each member of our family better." She says it is vital for them all to "push themselves further." And there is no doubt that, when the time comes, the family will get behind her, some will perhaps even be at her side to help her and ensure the handover goes smoothly. Margot remembers Claude as an "imposing patriarch," whose example she would love to follow. "He was so talented when he worked here." His granddaughter says that "it is difficult to fight against something that is part of you." She cannot deny that passementerie is in her blood. And although her admiration for Claude is undeniable, she has to admit that the world has changed since his time, and today passementerie has to write a new chapter in its story…

Margot Declercq knows that her mission is to usher Declercq Passementiers into this new era. Soon it will be up to her to expand the teams again and work with craftspeople from her own generation—because, for Declercq to remain Declercq, nothing needs to change, but everything must adapt.

Raw materials

The passementier buys raw threads (silk, cotton, wool, or fibranne) from spinners and gold threads from gilders. He has them dyed by a professional. Perfectionists, like father like son, the Declercqs have their threads specially dyed to achieve the desired color, so that it is as close a match as possible to the shades required for their restorations or creations. The House is particularly exacting about the quality of threads used.

Left: Spools of silk. *Right:* Skeins of organzine silk.

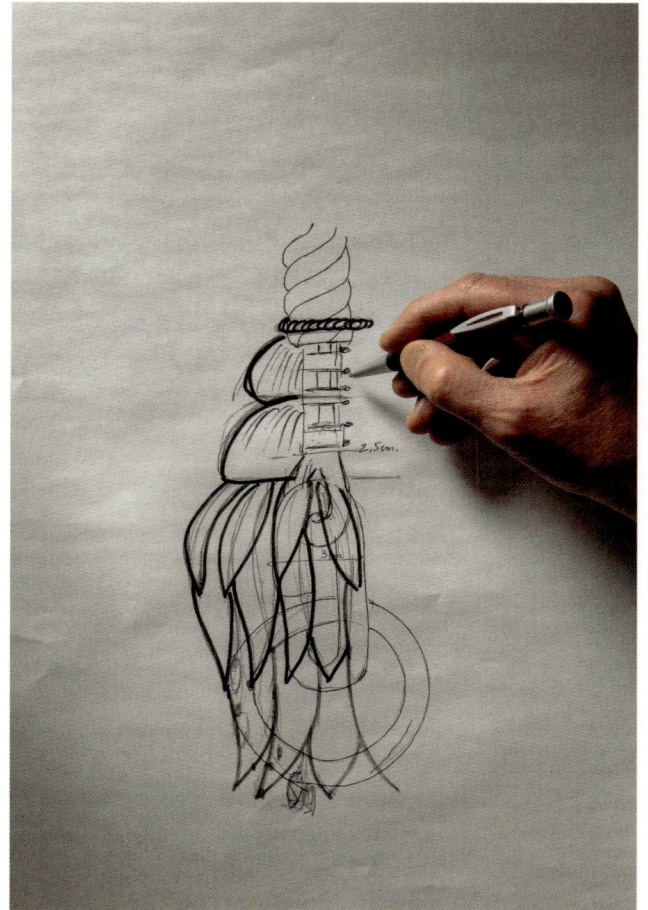

The production note

The craftspeople in the workshop are trained
on site so that they can work across multiple
disciplines, as each project will require different
amounts of work in different areas. The order
form and the production note provide an
important link between the workers.
These documents set out all of the information
and the work to be done at each stage.
The production note describes the design to be
created and the colorways to use; it details
which fabrics to use, according to color; finally,
it has a swatch of the relevant fabric attached.
It is important to match the colors exactly,
to achieve the precise shades so that everything
goes together. The note must be written
very carefully and precisely, drawing on an
understanding of the entire production process.

Declercq
Passementiers

Musée de
Condé
Chantilly

During this stage, armed with the production note, the worker chooses the necessary materials for each order. She takes out threads in the required materials, thickness, and colors, according to how they will be used for the weft. The colors and bobbins are laid out in order, following the design that is being reproduced as closely as possible. Often it is a question of interpretation, and it is therefore vital to learn how to look closely, to understand the subtle relationships between colors. It is important to work in natural light and to select threads when the daylight is at its best. If there is no thread in the required shade in stock, the worker prepares a raw skein to be sent away for dyeing.

Selecting threads

Top left: Thread color guide. *Right:* Choosing thread in the right colors.

Winding

At Declercq, we also call this stage the "potter's wheel." It is where the dyed skein of thread is transferred onto different bobbins, reels, or cones. But first it must be made flexible using a special machine, a long horizontal beam with wheels. The skein is wound onto the wheels, which the worker spins round and taps to separate the threads.

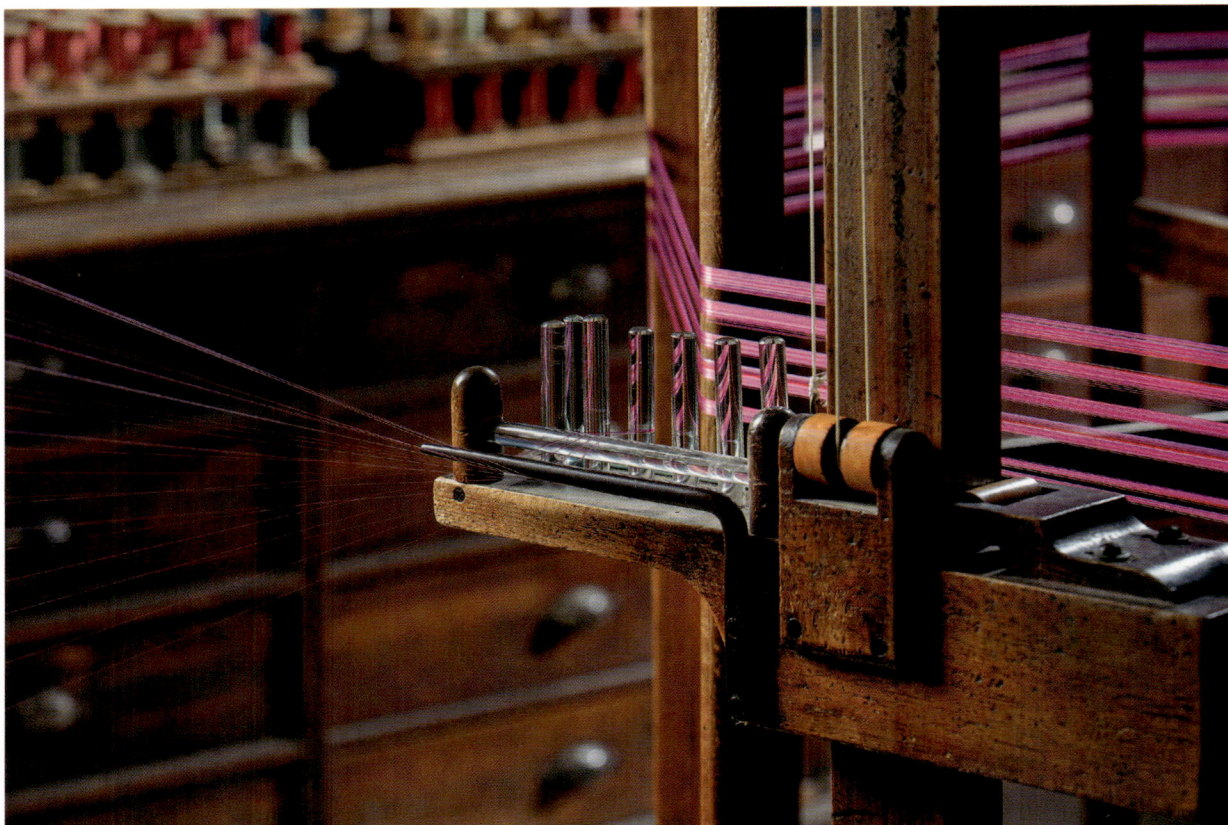

Warping

Warping consists of preparing the threads
on the loom, arranging and placing them so
that the warp can then be woven without any
issues, following the pattern set out beforehand.
"Attaching the threads is an art in itself. You need
to have the right technique, the right touch.
You have to imagine that what we are making will
need to last at least two hundred years," explains
Dominique, who has worked at Declercq for
thirty-five years. "The most important thing is to
love what you do, to have a feel for it, and above
all an eye. And also to let yourself take a break
every now and again, to work on something else
so that you can come back to your work
with fresh eyes."

Top: The warping machine. *Right:* Dominique at work on the warping machine.

The cards piano

First, the design to be woven is transferred onto
a piece of gridded paper and translated into
standard symbols. This determines all of the work
to come. It sets out where to punch holes
in the sheets of card, which will then be laced
together in sequence. These cards are then placed
on the Jacquard machine, in the "lantern," which
automatically rotates. Then it is down to the hooks,
rods, and individual warp threads, which cross
over, are raised up, or stay still, calling the shots
to recreate the required pattern as faithfully
as possible.

Above: Checkered braid and braid with wave design, in the Secession style. *Right:* Cards.

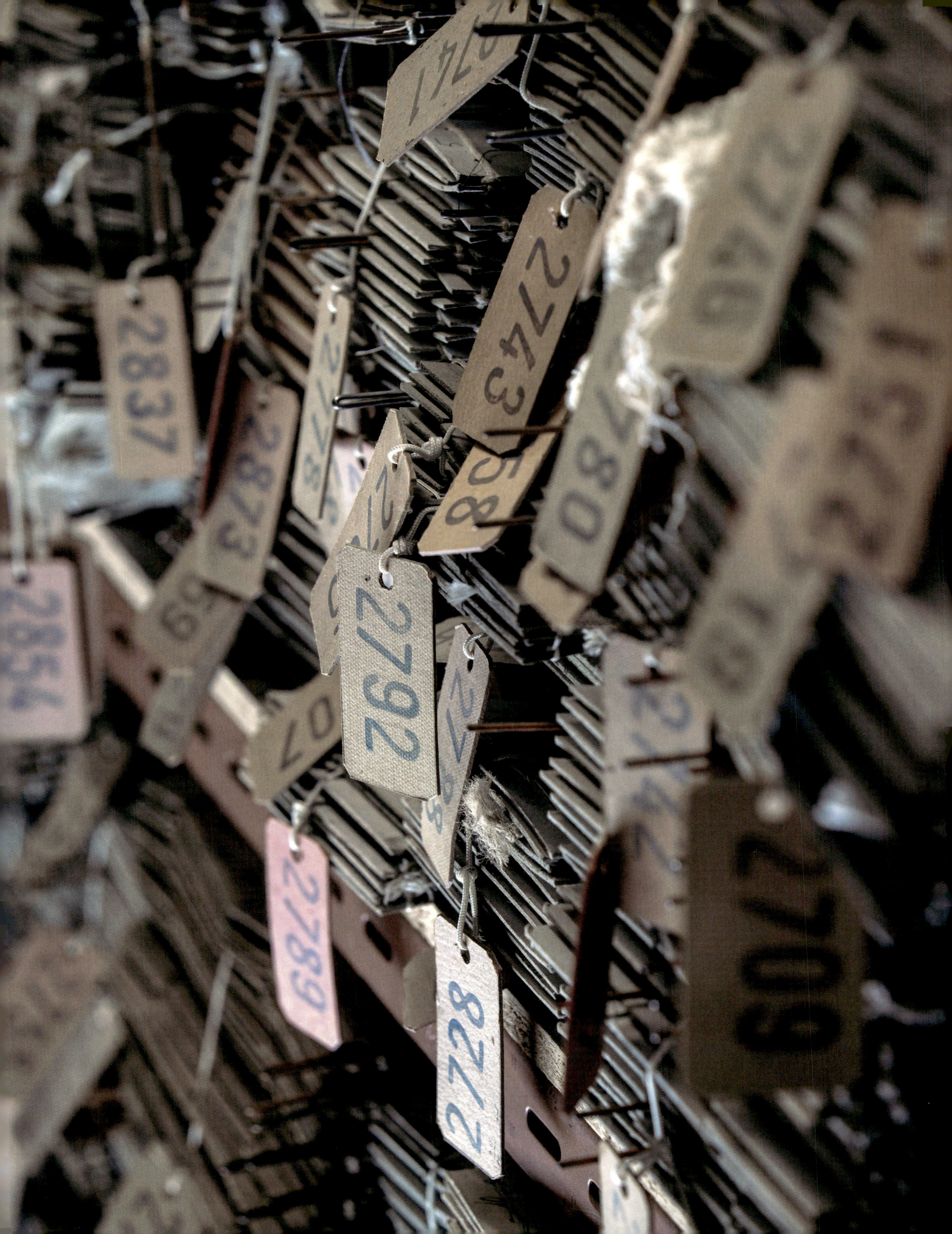

THE CHÂTEAU OF VAUX-LE-VICOMTE

◆

Built for Nicolas Fouquet,
Louis XIV's Superintendent of Finances,
the Château of Vaux-le-Vicomte—now owned
by the Marquis of Vogüé—is the largest private
historic monument in France. It is also famous
for inspiring the Château of Versailles.
In the King's Chamber, the silks and
passementerie, especially the fringes made of
silk and real gold, add to the majestic feel.

THE KING'S BEDCHAMBER.
Curtain with a border of gold braid. Fabrics by Le Manach. Embroidery by Lesage. Upholstery by Cousins
Associés. *Following page, left:* Gimp with a woven diagonal design, on the inside of the bed's canopy.

The loom

In passementerie, the most widely used weaving
technique is the Jacquard machine. It works on
the same principle as a barrel organ: perforated
cards hung on a Jacquard machine (made up of rods
that pass through the card if there is a hole and
are pushed in if there is not) and laced together.
The machine determines which threads will be raised
or lowered according to the pattern on the card.
Setting up the threads is one of the longest stages,
as the process has not changed over the years.
No one in the workshop could forget weaving
a double gimp on a Jacquard machine that dates
to 1887 for the collection "Les Ors."

Above left: Faycel setting up the looms. *Above right:* Jacquard machine. *Following double page, left:* Wooden creel for
a velvet loom; *right:* Detail of the heddles.

Twisting

This is a key part of the production process. Without it, nothing can be made. Everything that the workshop creates passes through this stage, which requires a great deal of dexterity. You need to have a feel for the material, to rub it between your fingers and hear the sound it makes, or feel it grow warm to the touch, to pay close attention, and remain focused. To ensure that the cord is evenly wrapped, Ismaël and Olivier have to maintain a steady rhythm. To find the right speed, the right pace. If they go too fast, they won't wrap it all, and it will snag, but if they go too slowly, they will create overloads, bunching. They can also use a rigid guide to control the position of the wrapping thread, according to the size of the cord that needs to be created.

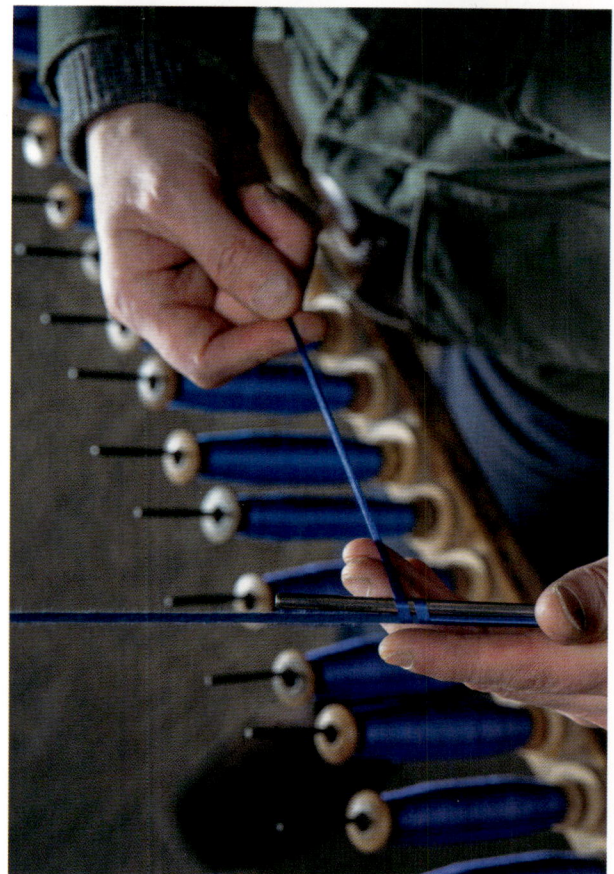

Left: Twisting wheel. *Above:* Ismaël with his "hand," the belt holding the reels of thread.
Following double page, left: Making torsades; *right:* Bullion fringe in progress.

129

Left: Making torsades on the wheel. *Above:* A "hand" used for twisting.

Mathieu Lehanneur

Designer

"I first met the teams at Declercq a few years ago, with the aim of developing a new way of thinking about passementerie. I discovered a story of craftsmanship that went back many centuries but now embraced a contemporary feel, looking to the present. Their approach to creating passementerie brings together our cultural heritage and our future. The project *Twisted Infinity* is a perfect example of this: a ring of light, almost intangible, woven into a piece of silk passementerie… Declercq Passementiers is eternal because, more than anyone else, these craftspeople play with history and time."

Twisted Infinity, designed by Mathieu Lehanneur.

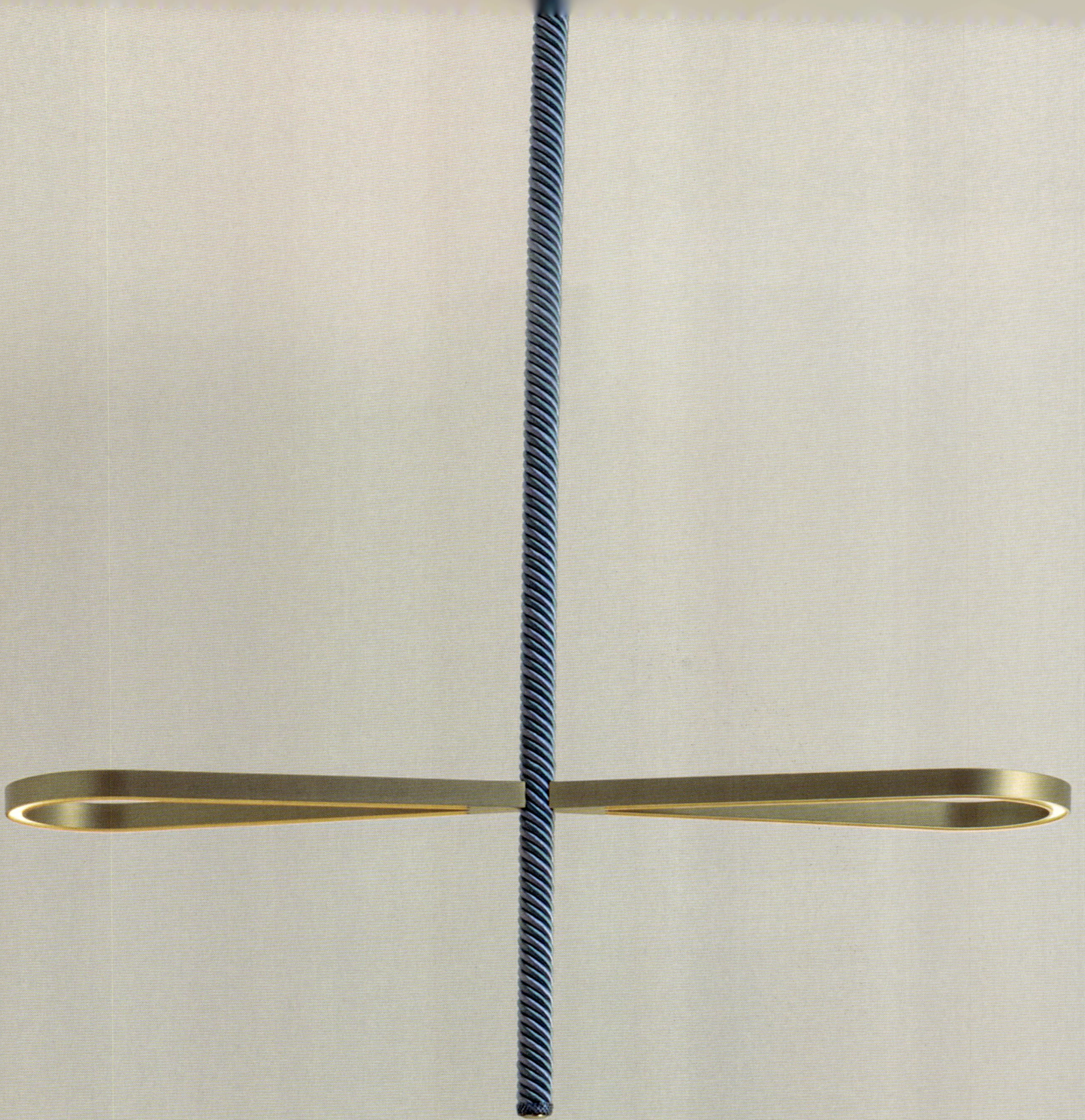

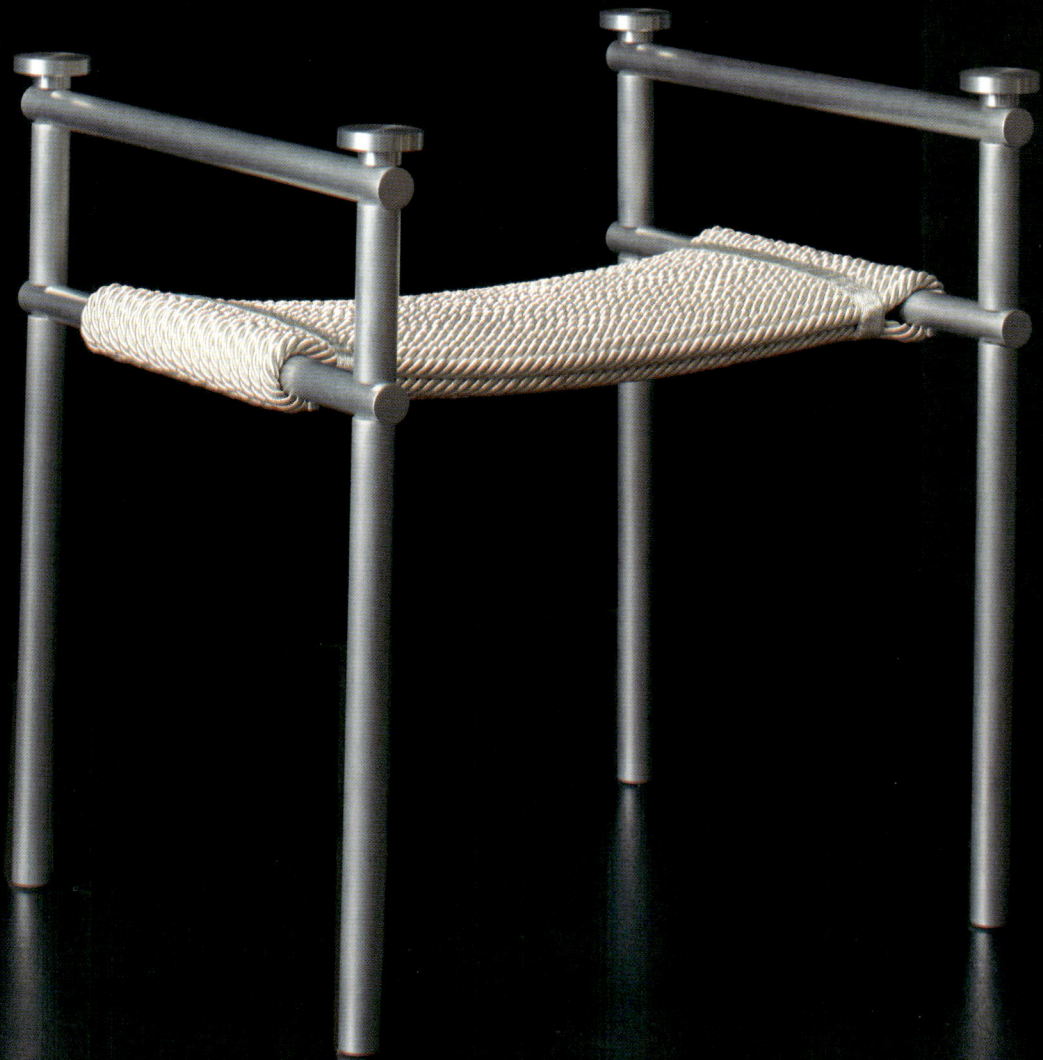

Edgar Jayet

Interior designer

After making his breakthrough in 2021 at the Design Parade Toulon, where he won the Van Cleef & Arpels Prize, Edgar Jayet launched his first collection in 2023 in Brussels and Milan, with the design Faudesteuil, created by combining different traditional crafts. In this piece—a stool—the aluminum frame created by Atelier François Pouenat showcases the structural function of passementerie, with the clever, three-dimensional use of rope to create a lightweight seat, while the finishing touches were made by Maison Brazet. "François Pouenat was the first person to have faith in me," says the young designer. He goes on to explain that, in 2021, he was able to realize his dream of working on his first project with this iconic House. Shortly afterward, he started collaborating with Declercq Passementiers, and the timeless lines of Faudesteuil were born.

"Although it is important to be radical, at heart I want to be part of a certain continuity, not to create something from nothing in order to invent a piece of contemporary furniture. I am thinking long-term, about taking the scenic route rather than the highway. Therefore, depending on the project, I play around with different time periods and, in my role as a set designer, I am looking for a space that gives me this freedom to create my own narrative. It is amazing to be able to work with such inspiring studios, where their creative work is enriched by being made in settings that are so full of history. For me, it is important to draw on these references. The rope supplied by Declercq Passementiers, which was created by Ismaël in Montreuil-aux-Lions, draws on this history of mentoring, which is as old as time. It gives my work greater depth and facilitates an exchange of ideas. Each one of these three Houses, which have similar histories, offers a unique level of excellence and I am very proud of these collaborations."

Edgar Jayet's Faudesteuil.

The braider

The braider is the machine used to create
cords with a cover that is braided on a spindle.
This is loaded with strings that interweave
to create the final cord.

Nelly working at the braider.

Hand weaving

On the hand loom, the weaver (traditionally
this work was done by men) operates the shuttle,
shaft, and harness cords, creates knots and loops,
and, at the same time, operates the treadles.
He is held in place by two leather straps, which
allow him to view his work from above and
maintain a high level of precision.
The hand loom is used to make complex designs:
gimps, double gimps with knots, braids, plaited
braids, bullion fringes, velvet sheared braids,
and fine fringes, as well as many others.

Right: Beams and sun-shaped loom.

Above: Jérôme Declercq working on the vertical loom. *Right:* Gimps for embellishing chairs.

THE HÔTEL DE LA MARINE

◆

In 1799, the Ministry of the Navy moved into the palace that held the Crown's furniture store, and it did not leave the place de la Concorde until 2015. The Center for National Monuments then launched a wide-ranging restoration project to return the quartermasters' apartments to their eighteenth-century glory.

This work, carried out by Joseph Achkar and Michel Charrière, celebrates the furniture fabrics, the wallpapers—some of which are original, others which have been artificially aged or burnished—and passementerie created by master craftspeople, faithful reproductions of designs found in Declercq's archives.

Bell-pull tassel. Fabric by Tassinari and Chatel.

PIERRE-ÉLISABETH DE FONTANIEU'S BEDCHAMBER.

Left: Tieback with two tassels, embellished with flowers, buttons, and jasmines with loops and *migrets. Top right:* Bolster with rosette and tassel. *Bottom right:* Alcove hanging, double gimp and fine fringe with loops and torsades. Fabrics Tassinari and Chatel.

MADAME THIERRY DE VILLE-D'AVRAY'S BEDCHAMBER.

Left: Tieback with two tassels made of aged spun gold lamé, with criss-crosses, flowers, buttons, twisted fringe, and torsades. On the curtain, a double gimp with loops and *duchesse* design. *Right:* The bed. Fabrics Tassinari and Chatel and Manufacture Royale Bonvallet.

MARC-ANTOINE THIERRY DE VILLE-D'AVRAY'S GRAND STUDY.

Above: Detail, braided rope, loop featuring Milan stitch and *chardon* design in aged silk. Braid made of aged silver lamé.
Upholstery by Sébastien Ragueneau (beds), Phelippeau Tapissier (curtains), and Rémy Brazet (chairs). *Right:* Vase-shaped
tieback with Milan stitch. Fabric Manufacture Royale Bonvallet.

Joseph Achkar
and Michel Charrière

Interior designers

This unassuming pair carried out the exceptional restoration of the Hôtel de la Marine on the place de la Concorde in Paris. In this project, Joseph Achkar and Michel Charrière sought to breathe new life into reception rooms that had never before been seen. They devoted themselves to finding the "perfect touch" to elevate these refined interiors, in perfect harmony with the spirit of the place, with its soul.

"In the Hôtel de la Marine, an eighteenth-century house, we stripped away all the layers of paint that were hiding the original colors. Luckily we were able to find these colors and use them as our starting point. Next, we used eighteenth-century fabrics that we bought one by one and showed to Jérôme Declercq." Jérôme, they both say, has an incredible ability to be flexible. "This was an unusual project, because we had a very specific idea of how we wanted to use passementerie, especially braids, from the eighteenth century in this particular context. For us, the most important thing was to resurrect the rhythm and poetry of the space. Mixing designs and time periods was out of the question. We didn't want to do an approximate restoration. Therefore the passementerie had to be in keeping with the original colors of the paint. Working from documents in Declercq's archives, we had old pieces recreated.

We chose designs that had never been remade, according to Jérôme, who fully bought into our approach, to the point of burnishing the silver threads himself to achieve the perfect shade, not too ostentatious or showy. It was a wonderful experience for all of us. Jérôme had access to expertise that is now very rare, and he approaches his work with a smile and a sense of humor. We looked forward to every meeting with him to find out what he had created, the progress he had made. All the pieces were very successful and we were very impressed by them. Passementerie is a hidden gem in the world of interior design, a small detail, but you notice it straight away and then it is almost all you see. Declercq is a miracle of the twenty-first century and, more broadly, it is a miracle that, in France, we have preserved the craft trade associations. We work on projects in Italy where we don't find the same level of excellence. Today, we are still working with Declercq on a house in Newport, in the United States, which dates from the late nineteenth century. It's a different proposition, but the experience is no less interesting. The important thing is to have the courage to always seek out elegance, without forgetting a touch of modesty, and above all to strike the right balance."

MARC-ANTOINE THIERRY DE VILLE-D'AVRAY'S BEDCHAMBER.

Tiebacks with two tassels with overlaid shapes, round buttons, satin squares, and criss-crosses, with torsades made of fine lamé covered in silk. Silk Manufacture Royale Bonvallet.

Charles Jouffre

upholsterer

"You could say that our collaboration begins as soon as the client—or the person commissioning the work—sets out their request and their expectations. After this first discussion, together we draw on the in-depth knowledge of our craftspeople to determine the feel of the piece to be created, and we set out our road map. This way, most of the time, the passementiers come up with the idea and offer us bespoke options. But we can also come up with different interpretations. We both benefit from each other's expertise. We feed off each other's experience, and that allows us to create a strong proposition. Jérôme works on the more specific technical or esthetic aspects. I always say that it's as if we're playing a game of ping pong. I have been working with this studio for more than forty years. I started out working with Claude Declercq. He undeniably shook up the world of passementerie. It is not often that you meet someone with such a strong personality. Jérôme and I like to work closely together from the start. That allows us to determine the different stages of work for all the teams. And, for us as for Declercq, passing on skills is the very essence of our discipline, of theirs, of craftsmanship in general. It is an environment that embraces learning and precision, where, as well as expertise, interpersonal skills are essential."

Jouffre's New York showroom, designed by Garcé & Dimofski.

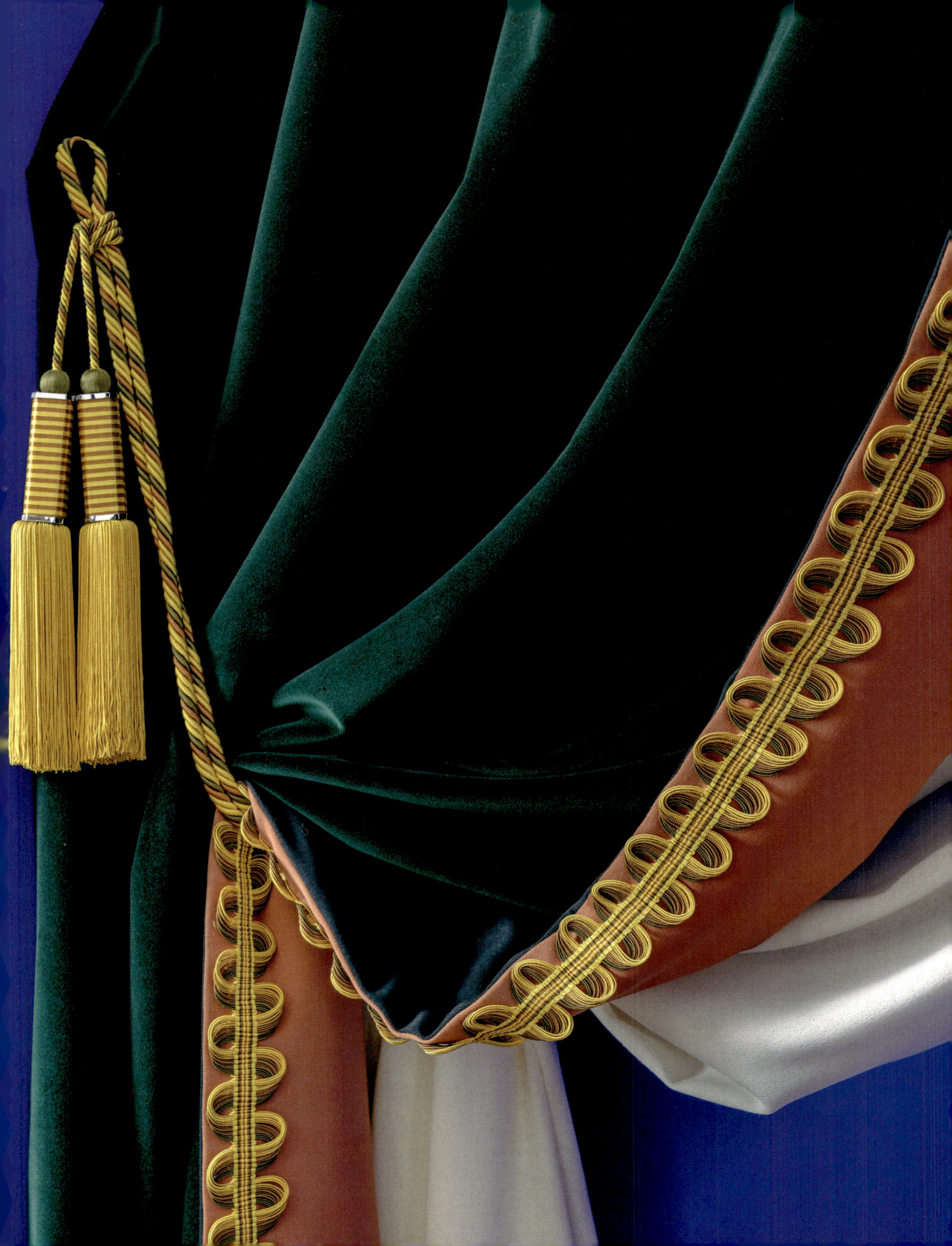

Molds

The place where the molds are kept has an air
of mystery, like a sanctuary. These wooden forms,
created by artisans using lathes, provide a
structure for the craftspeople's work.
They are used as stands when creating all kinds of
effects—*satiné, roulé, grappé,* and criss-crossing—
to ensure that the shapes created by the threads
are regular. They are used to create the tassels for
curtains or chandeliers, for example. The molds
are referred to by their shapes, with names
such as "onion," "olive," "radish," or even "tray."

Above: Ludivine wrapping a mold in satin thread.

Isabelle finishing a piece at the worktable.

Left: Loop and flowers. *Above:* The four stages of creating a criss-cross pattern using a Louis XVI mold. *Below, left:* Creating the flower's petals with a special tool. *Below, right:* Covering the flower in thread.

Anne-Sophie finishing a fringe at the worktable. The fringe features tapered jasmines, baubles, and long radish-shaped embellishments. *Following double page:* Detail of the head of a child's bed, with flowers and leaves made from card covered in silk thread and silk-covered baubles. Archive piece from the 18th century.

The other side of decoration

This piece brings together all the different skills
that go into creating passementerie.
Here the nine key stages are set out in detail.
This piece features a tassel with a variety of
effects—*roulé, grappé, coquillé,* and criss-crossed—
as well as a skirt of fine bullion fringe, a jasmine
with cannetille thread, swirls, padded leaves,
and silver torsades covered in silk.

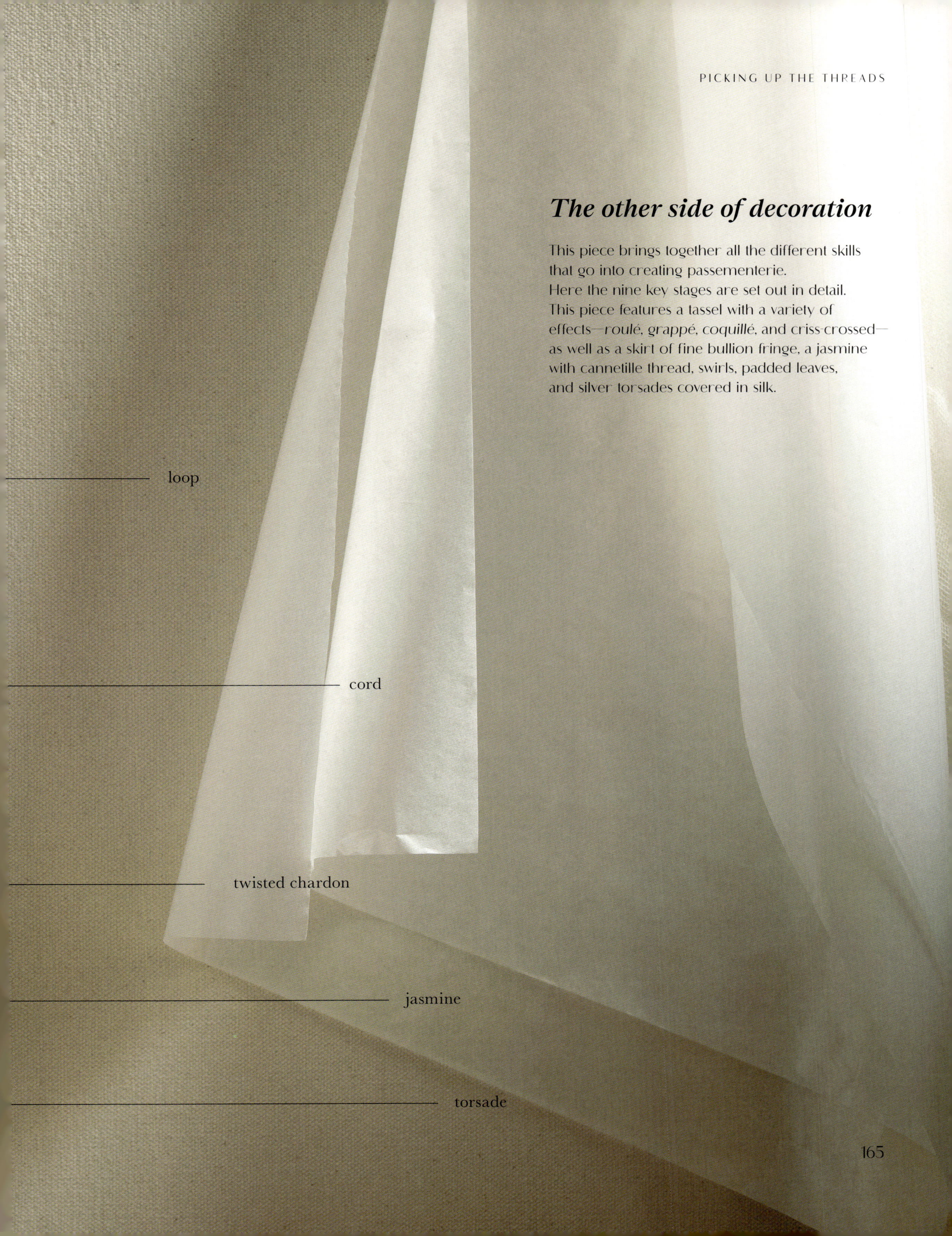

loop

cord

twisted chardon

jasmine

torsade

165

1. The **torsades** laid out flat, wrapped in two colors by the twister.

2. The **jasmine** is made up of many different elements, arranged in the shape of a jasmine flower: *migrets* (guipure with cannetille thread), padded flowers, and swirls created from covered rosettes.

3. The silk **cord** is made up of a number of individual cords twisted together.

4. The **duchesse** will be placed on the edge of the petals. It is made up of a cord (around the outside), a "core" (the center), and a trim that holds everything together.

5. The **cords** will be used to make the *grappés*, *roulés*, and criss-crosses. The threads that have been twisted together are placed onto bobbins.

6. The **wooden mold** determines the shape. The two fine cords frame the rosette in the center.

7. A small **garland** of flowers being created, using guipure and cannetille thread. A button is made of cannetille thread placed on a small piece of card, which is then filled using a bobbin.

8. A **rosette** with eight sections has iron wire inside to ensure it holds its shape.

9. A **loop** being filled, alongside cannetille thread.

Following pages: Decorative bows and rosettes.

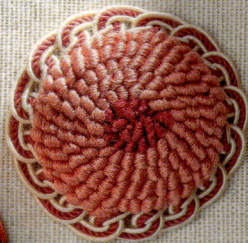

Previous double pages: Bullion fringe with diagonal design on the border, with torsades in two colors and cone-shaped torsades, jasmines with beads, baubles, and pendants, and jasmines with satin-covered beads with linework designs, satin-covered suspended molds, diabolo, and twisted satin-covered pendants with linework designs, some beveled, some rounded, on a Lampas fabric by Tassinari and Chatel. Designed by François-Joseph Graf. *Above:* Decorative elements created at the worktable. Cannetille *migret*, *limacé*, *grappé* mesh design, flower petals, leaves made from covered card. *Right:* Decorative silk-covered bow with a gimp border made from two types of guipure, buttons, and flowers with twelve petals.

THE CHÂTEAU OF FONTAINEBLEAU

◆

Napoleon's throne, in all its majesty,
is a stunning example of the wealth of furniture
from the First Empire that can be found
in the Château of Fontainebleau. Pieces that
survived the Restoration, the July Monarchy,
and the Second Empire, and that would,
over the years, cement the importance of
passementerie as a vital part of interior decoration.
In the early nineteenth century, there was
an upsurge in the different uses of passementerie,
as confirmed by the château's highly
detailed inventories.

THRONE ROOM.
Fabrics by Tassinari and Chatel. Upholstery by Rémy Brazet.

Throne with fringe of torsades and gold jasmines. Border with a diagonal design, fabric with bumblebee pattern.
Fabrics by Tassinari and Chatel. Upholstery by Rémy Brazet.

TURKISH SALON.

Left: Tieback with string of striped satin beads and loops, and rope made of silk and fine gold thread. *Above, right:* Gold and pale pink braid on a mahogany bed embellished with gilded bronze designs, acorn tassel made of gold thread. Figured gold lamé velvet by Tassinari and Chatel. Upholstery by Rémy Brazet.

179

THE EMPEROR'S BEDCHAMBER.

Above: Detail of a stepladder with a gimp made of silk and gold thread. *Right:* Detail of a fringe, with jasmines made from different types of gold thread. Marled silk velvet by Tassinari and Chatel. Upholstery by Rémy Brazet.

THE EMPRESS'S BEDCHAMBER.

Left: Empress Joséphine's bed. The bed hangings are secured by tiebacks with two tassels, jasmines, and gold stars. At the bottom of the quilt is a fine bullion fringe with jasmines featuring pendants and torsades attached to a double gimp with a diagonal design in silk and gold thread. *Above:* Detail of the tieback showing Joséphine's initial, in a round gold cartouche, surrounded by a green and gold torsade on a star made from covered card. Fringe with striped silk and long gold radish-shaped embellishments and silk wicks. Double gimp with knots and guipure made of silk threaded with gold.

Vincent Cochet

Curator of cultural heritage at the Château of Fontainebleau

The Château of Fontainebleau boasts a wealth of furniture from the First French Empire, which was in use to varying degrees during the Bourbon Restoration, the July Monarchy, and the Second Empire. It is essential to consider these collections as a whole and to think about how to present them from a historical perspective, in order to ensure consistency across all the rooms.

During the First Empire, craftspeople drew on decorative styles from the reign of Louis XVI, with an abundance of passementerie. The Second Empire proved less creative, but passementerie was still a dominant presence, both in terms of size and quantity. It was everywhere. It became an essential element of décor. The early nineteenth century saw an explosion in passementerie, which was used in a variety of different ways. However, its function was not only decorative. It had specific practical uses. Fringes were a way to emphasize the edge of a piece of fabric, while tassels ensured that a knot did not unravel. From these practical considerations, an art of ornamentation was born.

"When we start restoring a chair, first we have to consider it as a whole, to order wood, embellishments, fabric and passementerie at the same time. We are fortunate to have very detailed inventories. We know what date each object arrived at the château and what was delivered at the same time. We also have the suppliers' notes and, we must not forget, the objects themselves. We cross-reference all these elements to ensure our restoration is as close as possible to the initial design.

For the tiebacks, for example, we have a stock of old designs and we ask the passementier to recreate them. I start by sending them the original document, then I make my suggestions. For a gimp, for example: should it have fan edges, guipure lace or facettes? What width should the strip of glossy fabric be, in yellow, in pink… We have to be very precise. When we have recreated the passementerie for chairs where we are preserving their original fabric, the challenge was to achieve the same aged effect. The Declercq workshop had to dye the threads before weaving to create the mottled effect, to achieve the same color but with different intensities. They played around with how long the skein stayed in the dye to age the color and achieve different shades. It was when the threads were placed on the bobbin, when they were mixed together, that we found the perfect match for the original colors.

Our role is that of an interior designer. We have to think about the different groups and see the objects that we are working on as part of a whole. We also need to have a feel for how to mix the old and the 'modern', while respecting the object that we are trying to preserve. Consistency, quality, precision, being faithful to the original piece… these are the considerations that guide our thinking and our work. The idea is not to invent something new, but to stay in the background. Color, texture, playing with light, our work should blend in, to ensure that everything matches and nothing stands out. And the magic of passementerie is that we start with a thread and tell a story."

TURKISH SALON, CHÂTEAU OF FONTAINEBLEAU.

Tieback with two tassels, fuchsia-covered mold with green *grappé* mesh design, trim made of loops, strip of satin-covered baubles, jasmines made of satin-covered baubles, striped radis, and loops, attached to a mauve silk braid. Rope made of fuchsia and green silk. Handwoven double-warped gimp.

THE OPÉRA GARNIER

◆

Commissioned by Napoleon III as part of
Baron Haussmann's plan to transform Paris,
work on the Opéra Garnier began in 1860.
The first stone was laid in 1862.
The architect, Charles Garnier,
turned to the best craftspeople in France to build
this iconic theater, which was conceived as
an academy of music, choreography,
and lyric poetry. Made for the Emperor's box,
the gold passementerie gimps, recreated
down to the smallest detail thanks to Declercq's
carefully curated archives, are true jewels.

View from the Emperor's box.

Details of tiebacks in the Emperor's boxes. Fabric by Prelle. Upholstery by Jouffre and Phelippeau. *Left:* Fringe with close-set gold torsades and jasmines, gimp with gold lamé guipure tie. Tieback with two tassels, acanthus leaves and gold leaves made from covered card. Fringe of gold torsades and jasmines with gold satin-covered molds, leaves made from card covered in gold thread, and buttons. *Right:* Mold and leaves covered in a range of gold threads, and torsades with *chardons* made of torsades.

The Grand Foyer and its majestic tiebacks with overlaid molds, leaves made from covered card, *grappé* mesh designs, twisted fringe, and jasmines made from twisted pendants. Fabrics by Prelle. Upholstery by Jouffre.

Bouffette

Puffball created by gathering threads together, either cutting them short or forming them into loops.

Bouton (Button)

Round embellishment covered in thread in a cross-over design. Bordered with cannetille.

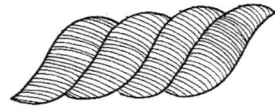

Câblé guipure (Guipure Rope)

Stiff rope. The threads are wound perpendicular to the core.

Câblé soufflé

Supple rope. The threads are wound parallel to the core.

Cannetille

Metal thread, covered and wound into a spiral.

Cartisane (Rosette)

Decorative rosette used as an embellishment on armchairs, couches, and cushions.

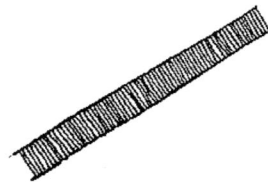

Cartisane (apprêt)

Strip of parchment covered in thread.

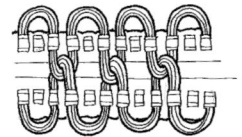

Crête (Gimp)

Strip of woven material, usually with an in intertwining pattern.

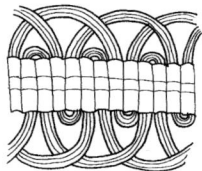

Crête giroline (Double Gimp)

Gimp consisting of loops.

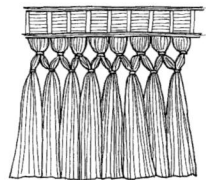

Effilé (Fine Fringe)

Fringe made from threads that have been cut off.

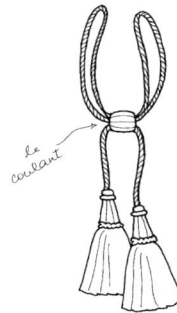

Embrasse (Tieback)

Piece of passementerie designed to secure curtains. Usually, it features one or two tassels.

Embrasse câblée (Rope Tieback)

Tieback made of rope (without a tassel).

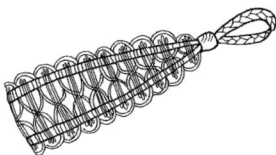

Embrasse crête (Gimp Tieback)

Tieback made of a gimp.

Frange à mèches
(Fringe with wicks)

Fringe that ends in wicks.

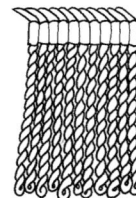

Frange moulinée (Bullion Fringe)

Fringe with twisted threads.

Galon (Braid)

Woven strip of fabric.

Ganse (Cord)
Very thin rope.

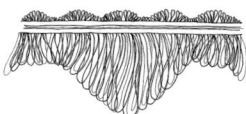

Giselle
Fine looped, scalloped fringe.

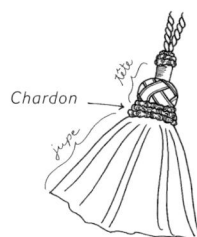

Gland (Tassel)
Piece made from covered and embellished molds, with a fringe at the end.

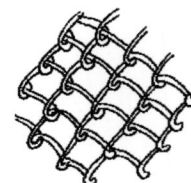

Grappé (Mesh design)
Mesh design created with a needle.

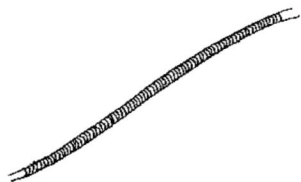

Guipure
Embellishment made from a very fine core covered with twisted thread.

Jasmin (Jasmine)
Decoration made from different elements threaded together (*migrets*, rosettes, bouffettes…) or from a torsade.

Jasmin de migrets
(*Migret Jasmine*)
Decoration made from *migrets* threaded together.

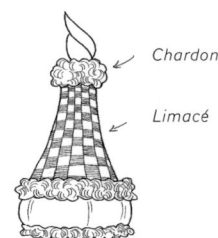

Limacé and chardon
Limacé: Stitch formed by a braid sewn onto a satin-covered mold to create a decoration.
Chardon: Embellishment made from loops of thread held together by a metal core and sometimes cut short.

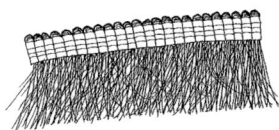

Marabout (Moss Fringe)
Very fine, dense fringe, looped and cut short.

Mèche (Wick)
Bunch of threads held together by a tie.

Mèches noisette et amande
(*Hazelnut and Almond Wicks*)
Bunch of threads held together by a tie. By varying the placement of the tie, these can form the shape of a hazelnut or almond.

Miroir (Flower)
Flower made from looped strips of cartisane.

Motif en remplissage
(*Covered-card Decoration*)
Piece of covered card with a cannetille border, used to create decorative bows, for example.

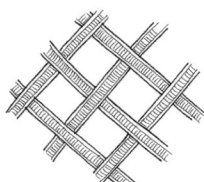

Passé à croix
(*Criss-cross pattern*)
Crossed strips of fabric forming a pattern on a mold.

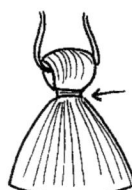

Postillon
Tie.

Satinage à coupons
(*Satin striping*)
Covering a piece in threads forming vertical stripes.

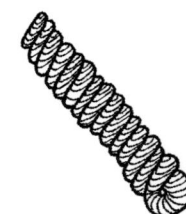

Torsade
Twisted metal thread held together by a core.

Left: Tieback with two tassels with glass beads, from the Metropolis collection. *Right:* Tiebacks with Ruhlmann beads, made from rare wood, carnelian, and stainless steel. Background painted by Stéphane Declercq.

This company's history has been written over the course of many years, through many encounters and friendships forged. As far back as I can remember, my grandmother and then my father worked very closely with leading interior designers: Robert Thibier, Henri Samuel, Monsieur Soutumier, Yves Taralon, Bernard Luthi, Robin Roberts, Bernard Gomond… As for myself, I have been fortunate enough to meet many extraordinary interior designers who have allowed me to write the next chapter in this story: Alberto Pinto, François-Joseph Graf, Juan Pablo Molyneux, Guy-Marie Kieffer, Philippe Parent, Robert Couturier, Jamie Drake, Thomas Jayne, Kazumi Yoshida, Sylvie Hendi…

Above all, I would like to thank the upholsterers who, working from a chair's wooden frame, a scrap of fabric, or a piece of passementerie, can create an armchair that will stand the test of time, a curtain that will embellish a window, a canopy under which kings and queens take their rest. I would like to pay special tribute to those friends who left us too soon, Jean-Paul Phelippeau, Gabriel Ravet, Xavier Bonnet, Josiane Fargeas, and Jean-Louis Babou, whose extraordinary work and beautiful character have been my constant companion and are still with me every day.

I would also like to thank all those who work with us: Alexandre Phelippeau, Michel Chauveau, Sébastien Ragueneau, Monsieur and Madame de Grandsaigne, Nicolas and Véronique Gheorghiu, Laurent Lachèze, Laurent Jannin, Isabelle Fargeas, Guillaume Viel, Georges Perrat, Frédéric Moulin, La Courtine… I love their work, the smell of their workshops, of horsehair, of fabric, and the sound of the hammer striking the tacks.

I would like to thank all those at Declercq Passementiers who have trained me and helped me throughout my career as a passementier. Firstly, Ghislaine Foucat, a wonderful friend, always loyal and ready to help, Lucien Hansen, Jackie Guillot, both exceptional hand weavers, Claude Leval, who taught me everything I know about weaving during my apprenticeship, Bernard Josset, who taught me the craft of twisting during my apprenticeship, and Paul Morgant, who has been a peerless studio director. Thanks also to Paul Dô, Pierre Thomas, Jean Gourdon, Jacques Rachel, Pascale Girault, Josiane Boudeville, Sylvie Moulet, Christiane Gorlier, Corinne Vessier, Catherine Magnier for her kindness and exceptional taste, Marisa Lopez for her technical skills, her eye, and her love for this family business.

My heartfelt thanks to all the craftspeople we work alongside, who give their time and energy to ensure that this family business can continue writing its story.

I would especially like to thank Inès Mathieu, whose enthusiasm and energy were vital to creating this book.

Thanks to Leila Boufaïed and Li Ti Kam Hà, friends and colleagues of my father's, who helped him to set up major workshops across the world. Thanks to Kapart for their exceptional work. Thanks to Arnaud Lebert for his support.

To all the châteaux, museums, national monuments, and institutions that have trusted us over the years: the Château of Versailles, the Château of Fontainebleau, the Château of Compiègne, the Château of Vaux-le-Vicomte, the Château of Malmaison, the Château of Chantilly, the Château of Azay-le-Rideau, the Château of Chambord, the Château of Champs-sur-Marne, the Château of Pau, the Château of Bussy Rabutin, the Châteaux of Grignan, Rohan Palace in Strasbourg, Schönbrunn Palace, Dresden Castle, the United States Embassy, the Quai d'Orsay, the Élysée Palace, the Louvre, the Georges-Clemenceau Museum, the Jacquemard-André Museum, the Nissim de Camondo Museum, the Museum of Printing on Cloth, the Magnin Museum, the Swiss National Museum, the Museum of Fine Arts Boston, the Getty Museum San Francisco, Legion of Honor San Francisco, the Frick Collection New York, the Opéra Garnier, the Opéra Comique in Paris, the Mobilier National, and the Center for National Monuments.

Thank you to the curators at these museums and châteaux, and to the architects and designers at the historic monuments who have allowed us to preserve our skills: Daniel Meyer, Christian Baulez, Pierre-Xavier Hans, Laurent Salomé, Bertrand Rondot, Jérémy Benoit, Hélène Delalex, Noémie Wansart, Monsieur and Madame Samoyault, Vincent Cochet, Bettina Caignault, Marc Desti, Laure Chabanne, Christophe Bottineau, Count Patrice de Vogüé, Élisabeth Caude, Mathieu Deldicque, Magali Bélime-Droguet, Étienne Martin, Liselotte Hanzl-Wachter, Sabine Schneider, Martin Chapman, Alain Charles Perrault, Agence Prunet, and Ulrich Leben.

I have had the privilege of meeting many highly talented people who have helped me to keep Declercq Passementiers moving with the times. I would therefore like to thank them for their boundless creativity. Alix de Dives for the incredible stories that she tells through passementerie. Roland De Greef, a loyal photographer and a friend of my father's, Christian Larit, a talented photographer and valued colleague, for the way he plays with light, his sense of humor, his unique pictures, and his incredible eye, and Alexandre Rety, whose pictures appear in this book. Thierry Guérin from Atelier 00, who brought his unique creative vision to the design and layout. I would also like to thank the press officers who have worked tirelessly to promote our family business in the media: Véronique Lopez, Christine Milou, Anne-Marie Mesnil, Valérie Ghérardy, and Éléonore Declercq.

Thank you to my family for their unfailing support: to my grandmother Nonna Jacqueline, who all our customers adored and called "Nonna," my grandfather Marcel, an exceptional businessman, my talented father, my mother for her love and care, Frédérique Declercq, who helped and supported me in my early years, Stéphane Declercq and Thuy Ha for their work on dyeing and colorways, Philippe Declercq for keeping an eye on the accounts and for his constant support, Elisa Declercq who is at my side through the good times and the hard times, Margot Declercq for joining us, bringing her joy and good humor, and for taking up the challenge of passing on our legacy to future generations. Finally to my wonderful wife, Éléonore, who creates remarkable work alongside me every day and who supports me with great patience.

Thank you to my children Amélie, Arthur, Camille, Margot, Pélagie, Célestine, and Colombe, for their unfailing love, which gives me strength every day.

All my thanks to those people, past and present, who make up the heart and soul of this family business. Our precious collaboration has endured through 170 years of history and will allow Declercq Passementiers to pass on our expertise to the generations to come.

Jérôme Declercq

With thanks to the generous sponsors who made this book possible

Ronan Allot, David Amiel, les Amis du château de Fontainebleau, Jean-Marie Apperce, Françoise Armstrong Declercq, l'Atelier Feille, l'Atelier Madame Fischer, Au Fauteuil d'Amour, Julien Aubert, Cécile Ayez, François Ballouard, Gina Barrett, Éléonore Bataille, Benoist-George, Franck Bernard, Maud and Franck Bernard Belloir, Jean-Jacques Berni, Jean-Marie Bertin, Franck Beune, Laurence Bischoff, Pierre-Yves Bischoff, Nicolai Bisgaard, Camille Blandin, Lydie Bol, Christine Bondu Chansard, Emmanuel Bosson, Alison Bouchardon Swartvagher, Nicole Boudet – Flanelle Décoration, Josiane Boudeville, François Bouvier, Olivia Boyer, Jennifer Brulfert, Pascale Brunet – Atelier Crépuscules, Helen Burzlaff, Julien Caillere, Lucas Canteau, Hélène Carlesch – Association Soieries vivantes, Sophie Carpentier, Nathalie Castagnet, Sophie Caux Lourie, Olivier Chadebost, Sylvie Chaigneau, Nayla Champagne, Kevin Chapuis, Stéphanie Chassagne, Laure Chevalier Sommervogel, Bruno Chevreau, Régine Pierre Chollet, Béatrice Cieslinski, Bénédicte Clergeaules Gammes D'Olbreuse, Louise Collombet, Philippe Coudray, Elsa Daillencourt, Chau Dans Mai & Mme Ha, Catherine Dartois, Isabelle Debouzy, Amélie Declercq, Arthur Declercq, Benoît Declercq, Brigitte Declercq, Bruna Declercq, Camille Declercq, Célestine Declercq, Colombe Declercq, Éléonore Declercq, Elisa Declercq, Florian Declercq, Frédérique Declercq, Jérôme Declercq, Jonathan Declercq, Margot Declercq, Pélagie Declercq, Stéphane Declercq & Thuy-Ha Bui, Titwane Anatole Declercq, Nais Deguerry, Raphaëlle Dejean, Étienne Delong, Marie Desgens, Coline Desire, Sylvaine Dominguez – Bagatelle Interiors, Christophe Duarte, Anne-Sophie Dutus, Ébène, Valérie Elaerts, Cho Eunjung – Dav, Fac Simili, Stefan Falsarella, J.-P. Farnault, Mathieu Fischer, Chantal Floor, Ghislaine Foucat, Stéphanie Fougerais, Frédérique Fournier, Ève Frament, Gildas François, Irène Galitzine, Caroline Garnier, Titia Gerritzen, Peter Geven, Véronique et Nicolas Gheorghiu, Ethel Gioielli, Muriel Goarin, Patrick Gouzou, Laurent Guelfucci, Claudie Guerin, Laurence Guil, Jennifer Gyr, Amaria Hadouch, Isabelle Hardouin, Anne Hauwaert, Valérie Huardel, Annette et Thomas Jacob, Mélina Jacquelet, Charles Jouffre, Ludivine Kaluzny, Peter Kammermann, Peter Kaufmann, Aurélie Kieffer, Catherine Kieffer, Florent Kieffer, Guy-Marie Kieffer, Hélène Lacourt, Héloïse et Yann Lancien, Charly Lavado, Raphaëlle Le Baud, Michel et Babeth Le Berre, Anne-Sophie Le Scouarnec, Alain Leblond, Virginie Legall, Florence Legaut Maringe, Emmanuel Lelièvre, Jean-François Lesage, Bettina Levin, Arnaud Levy, Catherine Leymarie, Stéphanie Lorenzi, Géraldine Lucchi, Sebastian Ludtke, Catherine Magnier, Christelle Maillard, Danielle Manie, Vincent Manod, Manuel Canovas Paris, Marie Luce Marchal, Francis et Jaqueline Marée, Maïté Mariana, Shona Martin, Bruno Martinon, Inès Mathieu, Mathieu Lustrerie, Yvette Mathieu, Stéphane Mauduit, Ainhoa Menchaca, Laura Menez, Agnès Meret & Blandine Bistoletti, Françoise Merlet, Marie Merlet, Sybille Messager, Melchner Midian Perret, Véronique Migeot, Milalou Luminaires, Cécile Moiroud, Corinne Montculier, Erick et Dominique Moquais, Rémy Motte, Jean-Denis Mouchard, Frédéric Moulin, Pierre Moulin, Marie Muller, Nathalie Naccache, Sonia Newell, Anne Nexoe-Larsen, Thu Huyen Nguyen, France Nicolas, Joëlle Nyffeler, Sandrine Orhand, Philippe Parent, Dominique Parnet, Véronique et Xavier Pascal, César Pazos, Andrea Perchtold, Fanny Perivier, Jocelyne Perruchas, Ludovic Peyvel, Alexandre Phelippeau, Laurence Pho, Ann Bruno et Constantin Porcher, Isaline Poux, Zak Profera – ZAK+FOX, Cécile Puche, Agnès Quere, Hélène Raimundo, Gabriel Ravet, Renaissance Tapisserie, Kamel Righi, Bathilde et Dominique Ropert, Nathalie Rouxel, Isabelle Rovero, Cécile Ruellan, Evgenia Shkirman, Nathalie Sibeyrand, Uwe Stein, Studio MHNA, Anny Tessier, Nelly Trehoux, Christine Tremon, Nina Troquenet, Truffaldino Décor, Lucie Vachez Collomb, Koen van Gestel – Trendson, Anke Van Goor, Philippe Van Mollekot, Joke Vandermeersch, Fabrice Vannier, Guillaume Viel, Hélène et Laurent Villemaud, Anne Villoteau, Alice Vrinat, Shinobu Watanabe, César Watroba and Laurence Zahner.

Left: First Empire ceiling decoration, with oak leaves and acorns made from card covered in gold thread.

Cover
© Alexandre Réty
Styling Aurélie Des Robert

Back cover
© Alexandre Réty

All photographs in this book are
by Alexandre Réty, except :

© Archives Declercq Passementiers,
photographs Alexandre Réty :
p. 30, 35, 36, 37, 39, 45, 47b and 51.

© Archives Declercq Passementiers,
photographs Alexandre Réty,
styling Alix de Dives : p. 33, 40 and 47t.

© Roland de Greef : p. 45 and 51l.

© Christian Larit : p. 19, 20, 21, 22, 23, 59,
60, 61, 62, 63 and 143.

© Jean-Marc Palisse, styling Alix de Dives : p. 57.

© Jacques Pépion : p. 4, 8, 9, 64, 67, 68,
69, 70, 71 and 180-181.

© Alexandre Réty, styling Aurélie Des Robert :
p. 16, 42, 162-163, 164-165, 166, 167, 168,
169, 173 and 198.

© Felipe Ribon : p. 135.

Rights reserved : p 49.

© Stéphane Ruchaud : p. 136.

© Sean Davidson : p. 155.

The line drawings in the glossary are
by Éléonore Declercq.

This book was produced in partnership with

Declercq
Passementiers

Editorial partnerships
Corinne Schmidt and Charlotte Court

Coordinating editor
Nathalie Mayevski

Graphic design
Laurence Maillet

Translation from the French
Bethany Wright

Proofreading
Nicole Foster

Photoengraving
Quadrilaser

Distributed in 2023 by Abrams, an imprint of ABRAMS
Copyright © 2023 Éditions de La Martinière, an imprint of
EDLM, for the original and the English translation

Printed and bound in Portugal by Printer Portuguesa
in August 2023
ISBN: 9781419767494
Dépôt légal: September 2023

Abrams. is a registered trademark of Harry N. Abrams, Inc.

ABRAMS
The Art of Books

195 Broadway
New York, NY 10007
abramsbooks.com